ESSENTIAL
GCSE PE

for Edexcel

Sue Hartigan

Hodder Arnold

A MEMBER OF THE HODDER HEADLINE GROUP

Orders: please contact Bookpoint Ltd, 130 Milton Park, Abingdon, Oxon OX14 4SB.
Telephone: (44) 01235 827720. Fax: (44) 01235 400454. Lines are open from 9.00–6.00,
Monday to Saturday, with a 24 hour message answering service. You can also order through
our website **www.hoddereducation.co.uk**

If you have any comments to make about this, or any of our other titles, please send them
to educationenquiries@hodder.co.uk

British Library Cataloguing in Publication Data
A catalogue record for this title is available from the British Library

ISBN-10: 0 340 90558 1
ISBN-13: 978 0 340 90558 6

Published 2005
Impression number   10 9 8 7 6 5 4 3 2 1
Year   2009 2008 2007 2006 2005

Cover photo from Michael Wong/Taxi/Getty Images.
Typeset by Fakenham Photosetting Limited, Fakenham, Norfolk.
Printed in Italy for Hodder Arnold, an imprint of Hodder Education, a member of the
Hodder Headline Group, 338 Euston Road, London NW1 3BH.

CONTENTS

ACKNOWLEDGEMENTS

I am extremely grateful to Jan Simister (senior examiner) for her help in researching and compiling this book and for her generosity with her ideas.

The author and publishers wish to thank the following for allowing use of copyright material:

Neil Tingle/Action Plus for photograph on page 2, 'goalkeeper' on page 30, 'female volleyball player' on page 31, Figs 2.3, 3.3, 5.11i, 7.2, 7.6ii, 7.6iii, 9.7, 10.9, 11.7iii, 11.7iv, 13.7ii
Martin Cushen/Action Plus for Fig. 2.1
Lawrence Manning/Corbis for Fig. 2.2
Image Bank/Getty Images for Fig. 2.4
Glyn Kirk/Action Plus for photographs of 'midfield player' on page 30, 'short and tall rugby players' on page 30, Figs 2.9, 5.1, 5.4, 5.5, 5.7, 5.9i, 5.9iii, 5.10i, 5.11ii, Table 6.3 'Ectomorph', Table 6.3 'Mesomorph', 7.3, 7.7, 7.8iii, 7.8iv, 7.8v, 8.2, 8.3, 8.7, 9.8, 10.3, 11.7ii, Table 12.5i, Table 12.5v, 12.3, 13.7i, 13.7iii, 13.9, 13.10
Richard Francis/Action Plus for photograph of 'junior tennis' on page 31, Figs 3.3 and 5.11iii, 7.5ii, 7.8i, Table 12.5ii, 12.5iv, 12.4
Steve Bardens/Action Plus for photograph of 'senior tennis' on page 31 and Fig. 3.4, 7.5i
Chris Barry/Action Plus for photograph of 'male volleyball player' on page 31 and Fig. 5.8, 7.4, 11.7i
Ed Bock/Corbis for Fig. 5.9ii
Mike Hewitt/Action Plus for Fig. 5.9iv, Table 6.3 'Endomorph', 7.8vi

Howard Boylan/Getty Images for Fig. 5.9vi
Owaki-Kulla/Corbis for Fig. 5.10ii
BDI Images for Figs 5.10iii, 5.10iv, 7.5iv, 7.5v, 7.5vi, 7.6iv, 7.6vi
Isaac Menashe/Icon/Action Plus for Fig. 5.11iv
Sean Garnsworthy/Getty Images for Fig. 5.11v
Tony Jones/Art Construction for Figs 5.14, Chris Blythe/Daedalus Studios for Figs 6.2 and 6.3
Koopman/Corbis for photograph on page 63
Bruce Burkhardt/Corbis for photograph on page 64
Corbis for 7.5iii
Warren Morgan/Corbis for 7.6i
Neal Haynes/Action Plus for Fig. 7.6v
Nick Laham/Allsport for Fig. 7.8ii
Science Photo Library for Fig. 8.1
Leo Mason for Fig. 8.5
David Nunuk/Science Photo Library for Fig. 8.6
Tony Donaldson/Action Plus for Fig. 11.1
Tony Henshaw for Table 12.5iii
Chris McGrath/Getty Images for Fig. 12.2
Scott Barbour/Getty Images for Fig. 12.5
Peter Tarry/Action Plus for Fig. 13.11
Adek Berry/AFP/Getty Images for Fig. 14.1

All anatomical drawings are by Tony Jones/Art Construction. Fig 5.3, 5.9v and 5.10v are © Sue Hartigan.

INTRODUCTION

The purpose of this book is to provide you with the information you need for the written examination in GCSE Physical Education. This book should also help you in planning your Personal Exercise Programme and increase your knowledge about factors affecting the sports performer.

In addition to learning the theory, if you want a high grade in this subject you must be able to apply your answers to sport. Try to practise doing this as much as possible. The book contains examples of how to apply your knowledge to get you started.

While the hope is that you will be interested in the whole book, if you are following the Short Course you will currently only be tested on Chapters 1 to 8, but please check as this could change. If you are following the Full Course, you need to use the whole book.

Exercise and Training

1

chapter one
REASONS FOR TAKING PART IN PHYSICAL ACTIVITY

GOALS

By the end of this section you should be able to:

☐ describe how physical activity enhances an individual's physical, social and mental well-being

☐ give examples of how membership to sporting clubs helps to achieve physical, social and mental well-being.

ACTION

List the reasons you have for taking part in physical activity (try to think of at least four reasons).

ACTION

Compare your list with someone else's in your PE group, and add any relevant different answers to your list.

Individuals join clubs and take part in physical activity for the benefits it brings. Probably the best way to understand this is to think about your own and other people's reasons for taking part.

The benefits of physical activity are normally grouped as follows:

- mental – to do with the mind, our psychological health

- physical – to do with the body, our physical health
- social – to do with the way we interact with others, our social health.

Very often benefits can overlap from one category to another. For example, if you were overweight you might take part in physical activity to lose some weight. This has an obvious physical benefit (you lose weight), but could also have a mental benefit (you feel better about yourself because you have lost some weight).

ACTION

Compare your combined list with the list in Table 1.1. This list was also created by a group of PE students. Are there any different benefits?

ACTION

Working on your own or with a partner, look at Table 1.1 and categorise each of the benefits as either a physical, social or mental benefit of physical activity. How many of the benefits could have appeared under more than one category? Compare your answers with those given in Table 1.2.

Reason/Benefit	Category of benefit
Lose weight	Physical
Relieves my stress/helps me to relax	
I need a physical challenge	
I am good at it	
Gives me better muscle definition	
Improves my health	
Gives me something to do	
Makes me feel good/improves my confidence	
I develop an aesthetic appreciation of the sport	
I like to compete	
Gives me a better shape/look good	
Makes me less tense	
Meet my friends	
Improves my fitness	
Stops me getting into trouble	
Good way of meeting boys/girls	
Helps me to learn how to cooperate with others	

Table 1.1 Reasons for taking part in physical activity

Reason/Benefit	Category of benefit
Lose weight	Physical
Relieves my stress/helps me relax	Mental
I need a physical challenge	Mental or Physical
I am good at it	Mental
Gives me better muscle definition	Physical
Improves my health	Physical
Gives me something to do	Mental
Makes me feel good/improves my confidence	Mental
I develop an aesthetic appreciation of the sport	Mental
I like to compete	Mental
Gives me a better shape/look good	Physical
Makes me less tense	Mental
Meet my friends	Social
Improves my fitness	Physical
Stops me getting into trouble	Social benefit, but not an individual social benefit
Good way of meeting boys/girls	Social
Helps me to learn how to cooperate with others	Social

Table 1.2 Reasons for taking part in physical activity

ACTION

Go back to Table 1.2 and try to explain how physical activity could bring about each of the stated benefits. Compare your explanations with those given in Table 1.3. Do not worry if you did not think of all the explanations. While these are the types of answers you will be expected to know, many relate to other aspects of the course so should be easier to understand once you have completed the other chapters in the book.

In your exam you might be asked to list some benefits of physical activity and categorise them. It is also likely that you will be expected to explain how physical activity actually brings about this benefit. For example, we have already seen that weight loss can be considered as a physical benefit; the explanation for this is that when exercising we burn off more calories than when at rest. If we had said that weight loss was a mental benefit, this would be acceptable provided we had a good explanation; eg as a result of losing some weight we feel better about ourselves.

Reason/Benefit	Category of benefit	Explanation (how benefit is achieved)
Lose weight	Physical	Doing more exercise than normal, so burning off more calories to reduce weight
Relieves my stress/helps me relax	Mental	By taking my mind off the things that are worrying me
I need a physical challenge	Mental	Mental – sense of achievement gained from doing something physical. Very important for those who do little physically during their normal day, eg people who work in offices. One reason why events such as the London Marathon are so popular is because people enjoy the physical challenge of training for such an event Physical – increase in fitness as a result of the additional physical work
I am good at it	Mental	Can improve people's confidence if they are seen as 'good' at something, especially if they are not viewed in this way at other times
Gives me better muscle definition	Physical	Through continued use muscles can develop strength and fat stores can be depleted (with an appropriate diet and training programme). Both of these factors would make the muscles easier to see (clearer muscle definition)
Improves my health	Physical	There are many possible health benefits to exercise, eg reduction in blood pressure, cholesterol, reduction in chances of weight-related illness
Gives me something to do	Mental	With something positive to do that you enjoy, you are unlikely to feel bored

Reason/Benefit	Category of benefit	Explanation (how benefit is achieved)
Makes me feel good/improves my confidence	Mental	You feel good for a number of reasons: you are having fun, you enjoy the challenge, you are not bored, and possibly because of the endorphins released when involved in long continuous exercise. Once you feel good, you feel better about yourself, and so your confidence improves
I develop an aesthetic appreciation of the sport	Mental	Most people enjoy watching a skilful performance and can appreciate the 'beauty' of that performance. This does not just refer to activities such as gymnastics or dance; it can be equally valid when watching skilful play in rugby or football for example
I like to compete	Mental	I feel good if I win; it allows me to focus on something else and use up some of my energy
Gives me a better shape/look good	Physical or Mental	Physical – this ties in with improving muscle definition and losing weight. Through using fat stores to lose weight and increasing muscle definition, the result is an overall better shape Mental – once I have a better shape I will feel better about myself
Makes me less tense	Mental	I relieve stress through doing a different activity, by taking my mind off my problems
Meet my friends	Social	My friends play the same sport as I do, so I see them at training or matches
Improves my fitness	Physical	Regular training will result in the body adapting to the new level of work we are asking it to do. These changes could include increased strength, increased cardiovascular fitness and many more, and are discussed in more detail in Chapter 5

Reason/Benefit	Category of benefit	Explanation (how benefit is achieved)
Stops me getting into trouble	Social, but not just an individual social benefit	By stopping me getting bored, and giving me something definite to do
Good way of meeting boys/girls	Social	Members of the opposite sex play sport, and it is a good way of meeting people with similar interests
Helps me to learn how to cooperate with others	Social	Through working with team mates, coaches and other members of the club I learn how to cooperate with others

Table 1.3 Reasons for taking part in physical activity

HOMEWORK

Interview people from other age groups and the opposite gender to you (these should be family members, friends, friends' families and peers at school other than your PE class) to see why they take part in physical activity. Categorise their answers as mental, physical or social and explain how these benefits are achieved. Present your findings to the rest of the group.

chapter two
HEALTH, FITNESS, EXERCISE AND PERFORMANCE

GOALS

By the end of this section you should be able to:

☐ define health, fitness, exercise and performance

☐ define cardiovascular endurance and cardiovascular fitness and explain its importance to health

☐ define muscular strength, muscular endurance, flexibility and body composition

☐ identify the relationship between aspects of health-related exercise and successful performance in specific activities.

There is often confusion over the difference between health and fitness. For this part of the course you need to understand these terms, define them and explain the difference between them. You also need to know the components of health-related exercise and their importance to sporting activities.

Health	Fitness

Table 2.1 Understand health and fitness

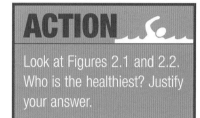

Health

According to the World Health Organisation, the definition of **health** is:

a state of complete physical, mental and social well-being and not merely the absence of disease or infirmity

(Source: http://www.who.int/about/definition/en/, 25 September 2004)

Not surprisingly, this is the definition that you need to learn for your examination. Note how the definition includes all characteristics of health, not just the physical freedom from disease. Think back to the previous chapter about the benefits of physical activity – the importance of exercise should be clear to you as it can have physical, social and mental benefits, all of which should have a positive effect on our health.

ACTION

Look at Figures 2.1 and 2.2. Who is the healthiest? Justify your answer.

Figure 2.1 Elite performer in action

Figure 2.2 Non-athlete – sedentary

People who do not take part in regular physical activity can still be healthy. They may have other interests to help them stay healthy, both socially and mentally. Through adopting a healthy lifestyle (balanced diet, regular sleep, non-smoking, limited alcohol consumption), they can still maintain their health.

ACTION

Look at Figures 2.3 and 2.4
Who is the fittest? Justify
your answer.

Fitness

Fitness is defined by the Edexcel examination specification as:

the ability to meet the demands of the environment.

This means that you are able to cope with the amount of physical work you need to do. (All subsequent definitions are taken from the Edexcel specification unless otherwise indicated.)

Figure 2.3 Elite performer 'at work' on the track

Figure 2.4 Non-athletes 'at work' in office

If someone is never expected to do any more physical work than walk to the bus stop, and they can do this without undue stress, then they are as 'fit' as the sports performer who trains regularly to meet the demands of their 'work'. The difference in fitness would only become obvious if the non-athlete were suddenly expected to do the same amount of physical work as the athlete.

QUESTION

Who is the fittest person in your class? How do you know they are the fittest? When does it become obvious that they are the fittest? Is the fittest person in your class also the healthiest?

Your answer to the last part of the question on page 10 may have been 'yes', but it may not have been. It is possible to be fit while not being healthy. Can you think of an occasion when this might be the case? Many fit athletes may temporarily be unhealthy if they are suffering from a cold or similar infection, or an illness like diabetes, or even in extreme cases, the initial stages of major diseases such as cancer. An increase in fitness does improve the chances of being healthy (see Chapter 5), but it cannot guarantee good health.

The other two terms in the title of the chapter are exercise and performance.

Exercise

Exercise is:

> *a form of physical activity done primarily to improve one's health and physical fitness.*

As you can see, this definition links health with fitness, recognising the benefits of physical activity mentioned in Chapter 1 – through exercise we can develop our physical, mental and social health and our physical fitness. A detailed explanation of the effects of exercise and training on the body can be found in Chapter 5.

Performance

The fourth definition you need to learn relates to **performance**. This is:

> *how well a task is completed.*

Performance can be anything from excellent to poor; it is simply a way of describing the quality demonstrated in a practical activity. We judge performances in gymnastics and diving, and how well a task is completed has a direct effect on the score for that performance. Although other performances are not judged in the same way (eg an individual's performance in a football match), how well they complete their tasks is still likely to have an impact on the final score, especially if we consider the team's performance, ie how well the team completed their tasks (eg attacking and defending).

Health-related exercise

In order to improve our health and fitness, we can exercise and improve the components of health-related exercise.

ACTION

Can you see any link between the terms health, fitness, exercise and performance? Discuss your ideas with a partner and feedback to the group.

Increasing our fitness should have a positive impact on our performance, provided we improve the right components of health-related exercise for our activity.

There are five components of health-related exercise:

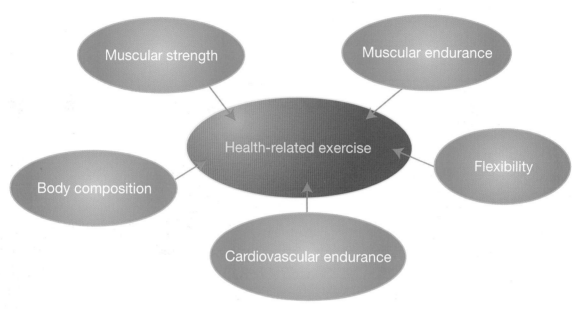

Figure 2.5 The components of health-related exercise

Cardiovascular endurance

Cardiovascular endurance is a very important aspect of health-related exercise. The definition you need to learn is:

the ability to exercise the entire body for long periods of time.

The cardiovascular system achieves this by supplying the body with enough oxygen so that it can continue to release energy, provided the intensity of the activity is not too great. For example, marathon runners are able to exercise their bodies for long periods of time (in excess of two hours), but you would not expect a sprinter to be able to sprint for the same amount of time. This is because their bodies do not have enough time to release energy using oxygen, as they are working **anaerobically**. This is explained further in Chapter 5.

Cardiovascular fitness is very important to a healthy lifestyle. The word cardiovascular can be split into two:

cardio and vascular

Figure 2.6 The components of health-related exercise

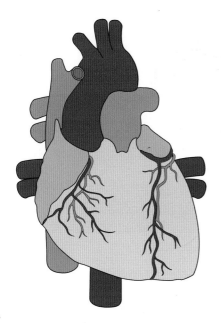

Figure 2.7 The heart

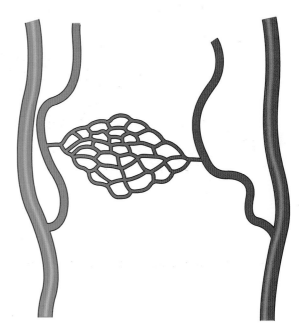

Figure 2.8 The blood and blood vessels

Cardiovascular fitness is concerned with the heart, the blood and the blood vessels. It is important to health, as there are a number of cardiovascular diseases that could result in death if left unchecked. High blood pressure, heart attacks and strokes are all caused by disorders in the cardiovascular system. Fortunately, a health-related programme of exercise can help maintain cardiovascular fitness.

Muscular strength

This is a very important component for many activities and is:

The amount of force a muscle can exert against a resistance.

For example, in cricket, the greater the muscular force (generated by using the strength of their muscles) the batsman uses to hit the ball, the further the ball should go. In gymnastics, gymnasts use muscular strength to support their own body weight in a variety of techniques and balances, eg a handstand, or a balance on the rings.

Figure 2.9 Elite gymnast holding position on the rings

Muscular endurance

This means:

> *The ability to use voluntary muscles many times without getting tired.*

Athletes with high levels of muscular endurance can repeatedly use their muscles to continue working throughout their events, allowing them to maintain the quality of their performance.

ACTION

Make a table and list as many sports as you can think of in the first column. Tick each of the sports that you think requires a high level of muscular endurance. Write a short statement to explain why you have selected each sport.

QUESTION

Why would a badminton player need high levels of muscular endurance in his or her arms?

Body composition

This is defined as:

> *The percentage of body weight, which is fat, muscle and bone.*

This refers to the chemical make-up of the body, in particular the amount of the body that is made up of fat compared with the amount of the body that is made up of lean body mass (eg bone and muscle). For example, if you weighed 63.5kg and had 15 per cent body fat, it would mean that your body had 9.5kg of fat and 54kg of lean body mass.

It is important to all of us to have some body fat, in order to allow the body to function properly. The percentage of fat that we have compared with lean body mass will have an impact on our performance in sport. Table 2.2 shows some percentage body fat scores for performers in different activities.

Sport	Male % body fat	Female % body fat
Baseball	12–15%	12–18%
Basketball	6–12%	20–27%
Field and ice hockey	8–15%	12–18%
Rowing	6–14%	12–18%
Swimming	9–12%	14–24%
Track – runners	8–10%	12–20%
Track – jumpers	7–12%	10–18%
Track – throwers	14–20%	20–28%
Triathlon	5–12%	10–15%
Volleyball	11–14%	16–15%

(Source: http://www.brianmac.demon.co.uk/fatcent.htm 25 September 2004)

Table 2.2 Percentage fat scores in different activities

QUESTION

Performers in which sport have the greatest body fat score? Which group has the lowest? Can you draw any conclusions about the relationship between the type of activity and percentage body fat? Why might it be an advantage in some activities to have a lower percentage of lean body mass (which weighs more than body fat)?

Flexibility

Flexibility is important to all athletes to differing degrees. It is:

The range of movement possible at a joint.

An increase in flexibility can help prevent muscle injury in some activities where the intensity of work can be explosive, eg in sprinting and football, and is very important in performers still in their teens as the body is still growing and developing. Increased flexibility in tennis players will allow for further stretching to reach the ball, but too much flexibility could lead to greater risk of joint injury as the joint becomes less stable. Regular stretching will increase the flexibility of a joint, although the actual shape of the joint (the way the bones fit together) will limit the amount of movement possible (see Chapter 12 for more information).

HOMEWORK

Learn the components of health-related exercise. It might help if you try to think of a mnemonic or a story to link the components. For example, the statement 'Buy, Many Football Club Managers (to improve health)' does not make much sense until you realise that it is one way to remember the initials of each of the components of health-related exercise.

- B   Body composition
- M   Muscular endurance
- F   Flexibility
- C   Cardiovascular endurance
- M   Muscular strength

This also reminds you that the statement is to do with health-related exercise and not the components of skill-related fitness covered in the next chapter.

ACTION

Complete the crossword opposite. All of the answers can be found in this chapter.

HEALTH, FITNESS, EXERCISE AND PERFORMANCE

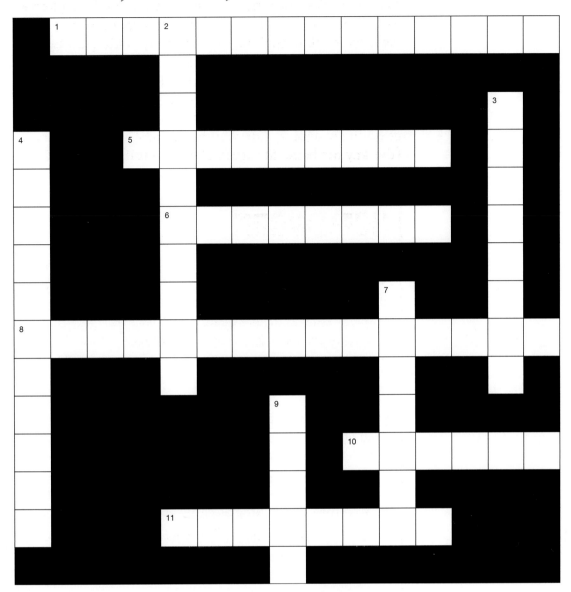

Across:

1 This type of activity is used to develop strength (6, 8)

5 Exercising without sufficient oxygen

6 Performers in this event need to make sure they develop their strength to help them increase the distance they can throw

8 What is the term that means the relative composition of body fat to muscle? (4, 11)

10 Sometimes confused with 7 Down, but refers to our mental, physical and social well-being

11 This is carried out to improve either 10 Across or 7 Down

Down:

2 Flexibility is very important to performers in this activity to help them achieve the shapes they need

3 To be good in this event the athlete needs very high levels of cardiovascular endurance

4 A definition of this term is 'the range of movement possible at a joint'

7 Sometimes confused with 10 Across, but means that you can meet the demands of the environment

9 What is the missing component of the cardiovascular system? . . . ., blood, blood vessels

SKILL-RELATED FITNESS

GOALS

By the end of this section you should be able to:

☐ explain the terms agility, balance, coordination, power, reaction time and speed

☐ explain how performance can be affected by these components of skill-related fitness.

As with health-related exercise, the components of skill-related fitness have an important impact on performance. All components are normally useful to all performers, but some are more significant than others depending on the sporting activity. The components of skill-related fitness cannot be improved through training as easily as the components of

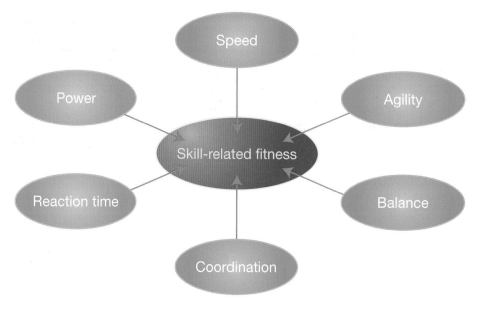

Figure 3.1 Components of skill-related fitness

health-related exercise; in fact, improvement in these areas is often due to anticipation and experience, rather than improvement in the basic skill.

As with the previous chapter, it might be helpful to think of a statement to help you remember the components (eg Mike **skilfully RAPS** on his **CB**). It is better if you can think of your own statement, as this will make it more meaningful and therefore easier to remember for your exam.

Speed

The differential rate at which an individual is able to perform a movement or cover a distance in a period of time.

Fortunately you do not have to learn this definition, provided you understand what it means. We all know that speed is to do with how fast we move, and we easily accept that speed is important to sprinters so that they can cover the distance of their race quicker than anyone else and win. But speed is equally important to a javelin thrower. Speed in this case refers to how quickly the thrower can move the arm during the throwing action: the faster the arm speed, the further the javelin should go.

Reaction time

Reaction time is:

The time taken between the presentation of a stimulus and the onset of a movement.

This is a very important component in activities where decisions have to be made quickly; eg when you realise your badminton opponent has just played a disguised shot and you need to move forward to the front of the court to retrieve it, or when the ball hits the top of the net in tennis and bounces off at an unusual angle. The stimulus is the thing you need to respond to, in this example the tennis ball; the onset of movement is when you start to move.

QUESTION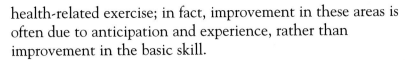

What other sports performers require speed? Give examples of how these performers use speed.

QUESTION

What is the stimulus for the badminton player?

ACTION

Give an example of the use of reaction time in an activity other than badminton or tennis.

QUESTION

Other than at the start of a race, reaction time is not so important for swimmers or track and field athletes. Can you explain why?

Balance

Balance is described as:

the ability to retain the centre of mass (gravity) of the body above the base of support with reference to static–stationary – or dynamic–changing – conditions of movement, shape and orientation.

Once again it is not necessary to learn this definition provided you understand it. Gymnasts obviously use balance to hold themselves still when performing techniques such as handstands and headstands. This is **static** balance, but other performers need **dynamic** balance. For example, for a rugby player swerving through the opposition en route to a try, or resisting a tackle and continuing on their run, and a hockey player changing direction at full speed, dynamic balance is critical.

Figure 3.2 Player maintains balance despite opposition trying to unbalance them

Agility

Agility is:

The ability to change the position of the body quickly and to control the movement of the whole body.

Figure 3.3 Discus thrower during spin timing movement of feet and arms to get more distance on the throw

Agility is about changing your direction quickly. Hundred-metre sprinters do not need agility in their event as they run on a straight track. Games players do need agility, as they are constantly changing direction to avoid being tackled by their opposition, or to put themselves in a position to tackle, or to move into space. Once again, the demands of the activity dictate which components of skill-related fitness are important to the performer.

Co-ordination

This refers to:

The ability to use two or more body parts together.

This skill-related component is obviously very important in physical activity. Activities that require the performer to strike an object, eg volleyball, require good hand–eye co-ordination. The body needs to be able to move the hand so that it arrives in the correct place to strike the ball, and it cannot do this without good co-ordination. Other activities, such as football, require good foot–eye co-ordination so that the foot arrives in the correct place to make contact with the ball.

ACTION

The performers in Figure 3.4 use the components of skill-related fitness in their performance. List the components they use and rank order them in terms of their importance to the activity. Justify your rank order.

Other examples of co-ordination include the combined use of arms and legs in sprinting to make sure the sprinter reaches the maximum speed, or the discus thrower coordinating his move across the circle and the movement of his arm to get the best possible speed, height and angle of release so that the discus travels further.

Power

Power is defined as:

The ability to do strength performances quickly.

Power is also expressed as an equation: power = strength × speed. To be powerful, then, you need both speed and strength. A gymnast uses power during the tumbling routine, where their movements explode from the floor. A tennis player will use power during the service when the racket arm is brought through quickly and with strength, so that the racket hits the ball with power to make the serve difficult to return.

Figure 3.4 Elite performers Mathew Pinsent and Steve Redgrave

ACTION

Complete Table 3.1 by selecting the important components of skill-related fitness for each of the activities listed. Give an example of how it is used in the activity.

	Hockey	Gymnastics	Steeplechase
Reaction time			
Agility			
Power			
Speed			
Coordination			
Balance			

Table 3.1 Applying components of skill-related fitness to activities

HOMEWORK

Think about the activities for which you are being assessed in your practical work. What are the important components of skill-related fitness for these activities? How do they help your performance?

chapter four
PRINCIPLES OF TRAINING

? QUESTION

Which principles of training are represented by SPORT?

S ➡

P ➡

O ➡

R ➡

T ➡

Fill in the missing principles of training.

M ➡

F ➡

I ➡

You need to know about the principles of training because correct application of them within your PEP should lead to an improvement in aspects of your health-related exercise. In other words, they are 'rules' which, if followed, allow your training to be more effective; this should have a positive impact on your performance in whichever sporting activity you participate.

Figure 4.1 shows the principles of training that you are required to know for the Edexcel specification.

As with the previous chapter it might be helpful to think of a way to help you remember the components. SPORT is a well known acronym used to remember the principles of training, but unfortunately it does not cover all of the principles that you need to know.

So, we now have SPORT MIF, but we could mix the letters and use FIRM STOP or FORM TIPS (does this cover all of

Figure 4.1 Principles of training

the principles of training you need to know?). Better still, you could make up your own phrase; if you can think of a way to rearrange the letters so that it is meaningful to you, you are more likely to be able to remember it.

Remembering the names of the principles is a good start, but you will also be expected to define some, explain what all of them mean, recognise them from their description or definition and show how you might apply them in a personal exercise programme (PEP) to improve aspects of health-related exercise.

You should plan a PEP as part of your practical work. If your PEP is going to be effective in improving aspects of your health-related exercise it needs to be well thought out and continually evaluated to check you are doing the right things. Development of a PEP should go through the following stages.

Planning

- Identify your goals (what activity do you want to get fit for).
- Find out how fit you currently are (carry out some fitness tests).
- Identify your strengths and weaknesses (analyse your fitness test results).

- Select the areas of health-related exercise you need to work on (based on your goals and current weaknesses).
- Choose a training method to suit your goal (e.g. continuous training to improve cardiovascular endurance).
- Decide on activities and workload to suit your training method.

Performing

- Carry out the PEP sessions.

Evaluating

- Assess the session.
- Plan the next session (change workload, change activities as appropriate).
- Final testing.
- Final evaluation (did you achieve your goals?).

Definitions of some principles of training

Overload:

Fitness can only be improved through training more than you normally do.

Progression:

Start slowly and gradually increase the amount of exercise you do.

Specificity:

You must do specific kinds of activity or exercise to build specific body parts.

Although this is a recognised definition of specificity, it is not very clear. If asked to define specificity you should give this definition, but if asked to explain you should use a different word from 'specific' to demonstrate that you understand the principle.

Overload

What training do you currently do? If you wanted to apply the principle of overload, what would you have to do to the amount of training you currently do? Give a specific example.

ACTION

Look at the three definitions above. What do you think each one means? How might each one apply to you?

The critical part of the definition of overload is 'training more than you normally do'. This should make it easy to think of an example. If you currently train twice a week, you would be overloading by training three times a week. The reason for overloading the body is that by making it work harder it has to adapt to the new work rate, therefore making you 'fitter' (look back at the definition of fitness in Chapter 2). These adaptations are dealt with in Chapter 5, but the way in which the body adapts makes it easier for the sports performer to perform well. For example, a sprinter should run faster once their body has adapted to extra physical work, because they are becoming more muscular.

QUESTION ?

How would you apply overload in the examples given in Table 4.1?

Example	Application of Overload
Train twice a week	
Work for 30 minutes	
Complete 25 repetitions	
Lift 5 Kg	
Work at 70% of my maximum heart rate	

Table 4.1 Applications of overload

Progression

The critical part of this definition is 'gradually increase the amount of exercise'. Progression is obviously very similar to the principle of overload. Both state that you should work the body harder. The difference is that progression controls the rate at which you increase the workload.

Which of the examples in Table 4.2 demonstrate the principle of progression?

Example	Progression	Accurate application of progression – Yes/No?
Train twice a week	Train five times a week	
Work for 30 minutes	Work for 31 minutes	
Complete 25 repetitions	Complete 30 repetitions	
Lift 5 Kg	Lift 4 Kg	
Work at 70% of my maximum heart rate	Work at 75% of my maximum heart rate	

Table 4.2 Applying progression

? QUESTION

Why do you think we need progression as well as overload?

Specificity

This principle is stating that you cannot just do any type of training, but that you must match your training to the needs of your sport.

Would you expect the pairs of athletes in Table 4.3 to follow the same training programme? If not, why not?

Pairs of Athletes		Same PEP – Yes/No?
Sprinter	Marathon runner	
Netball player	Swimmer	
Dancer	Squash player	
Tennis player	Rugby player	
Footballer	Footballer	

Table 4.3 Training needs

Explanations of Principles of Training

Remember that a definition is asking for something very specific, normally an exact repeat of a statement from the specification. Explanations are different. They are your interpretation of a definition. They should be in your own words, but still give the meaning of the term you are being asked to explain.

Individual needs

This principle of training is similar to the principle of specificity. The difference is that this principle considers the needs of the individual, rather than the needs of the sporting activity. In other words, according to the principle of specificity, two footballers could do the same training programme. (Consider Rio Ferdinand and Michael Owen, or any other two performers. Would you give them the same training programme?) By adding the principle of individual needs we should formulate a much better PEP, as the training will also consider the performer. Factors such as age, sex, sporting experience, weight, height, current level of fitness should all make a difference to the type of training programme followed. If you consider these things when forming your own PEP, then you are applying the principle of individual needs.

Reversibility

You would not willingly apply this principle to your training. It describes what happens to your levels of fitness if you have a break in your training because of an injury, a holiday, because it is the end of the season, or because you do not want to train anymore. In the same way that your body adapts to an increased level of physical work, it will readapt to a lower level of physical work.

Thresholds of training

This principle links with the principle of overload. The principle of overload says that you should increase the amount of physical work that you do in order to increase fitness, but how much of an increase do you need in order to be effective and safe? The principle of progression says that this increase should be gradual, but still does not give us a clear guideline as to how hard we should work.

Thresholds of training give clear guidelines for safe working levels (provided the individual is healthy). It is suggested that the average performer should train between 60 and 80 per cent of their maximum heart rate, although elite performers will often train outside of this range. Figure 5.12 in the next chapter shows the minimum and maximum thresholds for different age groups.

ACTION

You should be able to explain the principles of overload, progression and specificity from the work you have already done. Either write down or explain to a partner each of these principles. Compare your explanation with your partner's. Are they the same? If they are different, can they both be correct?

QUESTION

If your body becomes fitter as a result of extra physical work in training, what is likely to happen to your level of fitness if you do less physical work?

ACTION

Consider the pairs of images in Table 4.4 on pages 30 and 31. Under the 'rule' of the principle of individual needs and/or specificity, decide if any of these performers could use the same training programme. Justify your answer.

Yes/No

Justification

Yes/No

Justification

Midfield player

Football goalkeeper

Two international rugby players, different body weights and size and positions

Justification

Male volleyball player

Yes/No **Justification**

Senior tennis

Female volleyball player

Junior tennis

Table 4.4 Individual training needs

Moderation

As the name of the principle suggests, this is concerned with doing enough training, but not too much.

QUESTION

Which principles would moderation link with?

FITT principle (Frequency, Intensity, Time, Type)

This is the last of the principles that you need to know. The FITT principle is used to increase the amount of physical work the body does, in other words, how you achieve overload. The first three letters in the principle are ways of achieving overload, and the fourth letter is a reminder that the overload needs to be specific to the activity for which you are training.

According to this principle, you work harder than before but within your target zone, gradually increasing the amount of work you do.

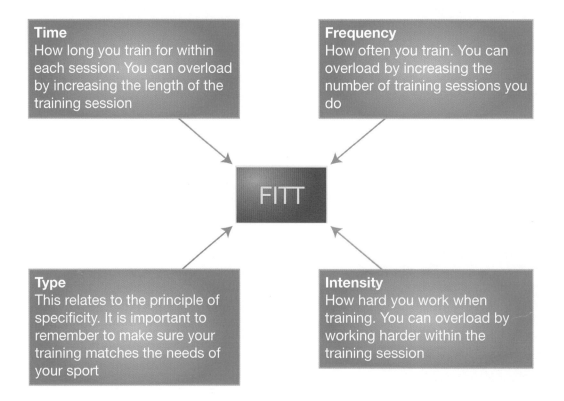

Time
How long you train for within each session. You can overload by increasing the length of the training session

Frequency
How often you train. You can overload by increasing the number of training sessions you do

FITT

Type
This relates to the principle of specificity. It is important to remember to make sure your training matches the needs of your sport

Intensity
How hard you work when training. You can overload by working harder within the training session

Figure 4.2 The components of the FITT Principle

ACTION

Your target zone is different from your friends', some of whom play different sports. This week you trained for an extra session, although last week you made one of the sessions longer than usual. You think that you might work harder within the session next week, but you have said that you will be careful not to do too much because you do not wish to miss any training sessions through injury, as this could lead to a drop in fitness.

Which principles of training are being referred to in this extract?

HOMEWORK

If you have already designed a PEP, identify where you have followed the principles of training. Give specific examples of the weights used, or number of repetitions you complete. If you have not yet planned a PEP, consider some of the activities you would include, explaining how the principles of training would be applied.

chapter five
METHODS OF TRAINING

GOALS

By the end of this section you should be able to:

☐ describe the stages of an exercise session

☐ explain the difference between aerobic and anaerobic activity

☐ describe continuous, circuit, Fartlek, cross, interval and weight training

☐ graphically demonstrate and explain the use of target zones

☐ describe the immediate effects of exercise, the effects of regular training and the long-term benefits of exercise on the

   1 bones, joints and muscles

   2 cardiovascular and respiratory systems

☐ explain the meaning of recovery rates

☐ use all of the above to help you plan, perform and amend your PEP.

(Note that the difference between isotonic and isometric muscle contractions is covered in Chapter 13.)

The exercise session

Any exercise session, whatever the sporting activity, should involve a **warm up** before the **main activity** and a **cool down** after it.

There are good reasons for this. The warm up is used to prepare the body for the activity you are about to take part in. It should help you physically and mentally. The cool down helps return the body to a resting state. More information on the warm up and cool down can be found in Chapter 7.

Figure 5.1 Warm up → main activity (competition) → cool down

Aerobic and anaerobic activity

You need to understand the difference between these two terms so that you can recognise the type of activity you do in your sport. You can then match your training to the requirements of the sport.

In simple terms, aerobic means 'with oxygen', therefore anaerobic means 'without oxygen'. These terms relate to the intensity of the activity, or how hard you are physically making the body work. For example, the 100 metre sprint is an anaerobic activity because you work as hard as you can (**maximal** level). When we work at this rate it is not possible to supply the muscles with the oxygen they need to release energy for the exercise, so we work without oxygen, anaerobically, and repay the oxygen debt once the exercise is completed (see Chapter 10). The problem is that because of the lack of oxygen, we can only work at this level for a limited period of time, therefore longer events such as the 3000 metres are mainly aerobic.

QUESTION ?

If it takes an elite male 100 metre runner approximately ten seconds to run the 100 metres, how long would it take an elite 3000 metre runner to complete their event if they were able to work at the same anaerobic pace as the 100 metre runner for the whole race? (See Table 5.1.)

Event	Predicted time for event IF same pace could be maintained anaerobically throughout the event
100 metres	10 seconds
200 metres	20 seconds
400 metres	40 seconds
800 metres	1 minute 20 seconds
1500 metres	2 minutes 30 seconds
3000 metres	????

Table 5.1 Applying anaerobic rates

? QUESTION

Read Table 5.2 below. When do the events appear to change from anaerobic to aerobic?

Event	Predicted time for event IF same pace could be maintained anaerobically throughout the event	Current World Record (to nearest second)
100 metres	10 seconds	10 seconds
200 metres	20 seconds	19 seconds
400 metres	40 seconds	43 seconds
800 metres	1 minutes 20 seconds	1 minute 41 seconds
1500 metres	2 minutes 30 seconds	3 minutes 26 seconds
3000 metres	????	7 minutes 21 seconds

Table 5.2 From anaerobic to aerobic

An extreme example of an anaerobic activity is the 100 metre sprint. An extreme example of an aerobic activity is the marathon, although aspects of the marathon will be anaerobic, eg the sprint finish. Similarly, many team games will have aspects of aerobic and anaerobic activity within them.

? QUESTION

Is your sporting activity or your role within it mainly aerobic, anaerobic or a combination of both? The intensity at which you have to work should make a difference to the training method you select.

Methods of training

In the previous chapter you covered the principles of training. Once you understand these principles, you will be in a better position to develop an appropriate training programme (PEP) to improve your fitness and therefore your performance in your chosen activity.

This means that before preparing your PEP, you need to look at the demands of your sport carefully to see which of the components of fitness are most important.

QUESTION ?

What was the name of the principle of training which stated that you should match your training to the needs of your sport?

Sporting activity:		
Component of health-related exercise/skill-related fitness (see Chapters 2 and 3)	Is this component relevant to my sporting activity? ✓/✗	Why is this component is relevant to my sporting activity?
Cardiovascular endurance		
Muscular strength		
Muscular endurance		
Flexibility		
Body composition		
Speed		
Agility		
Balance		
Coordination		
Reaction time		
Power		

Table 5.3 Improving components of fitness

ACTION

Copy and complete Table 5.3 by selecting the component of fitness you want to improve to make you a better performer.

Now that you have a clearer idea about which aspect of fitness you need to improve, you need to choose a method of training which will bring those improvements. There are several different types of training methods. For this course you need to be able to describe the following methods and give examples of when they would be used:

- continuous training
- interval training
- circuit training
- weight training
- cross training
- Fartlek training.

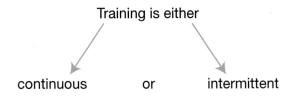

Figure 5.2 Types of training methods

In other words, you are either training without a break (continuously) or training with breaks during the session (intermittently). All of the other types of training fall under one of these headings.

Continuous training

This develops cardiovascular fitness and muscular endurance. As mentioned above, it is called continuous because you do not rest. It is an aerobic activity which uses large muscle groups; activities include cycling, jogging and step aerobics. Continuous training requires the performer to work between 60 and 80 per cent of their training threshold (see thresholds of training later in the chapter), for a minimum of 15 minutes (although longer would be more advantageous) at least three times a week to have any effect on cardiovascular and muscular endurance.

Circuit training

The principles of circuit training are as follows:

1. A number of different exercises are carried out at 'stations'.
2. Each exercise should be carefully selected to make sure that it is relevant to the aim or purpose of the sports performer's PEP. For example, if the performer were a

Figure 5.3 Set up for circuit training session

games player and they wanted to improve their muscular endurance, they would include exercises that related to their sport and this area of fitness.

3. The stations are normally positioned in a circular order and are completed one after the other.

4. Care has to be taken to organise the circuit so that different muscle groups are used from one station to the next.

5. The performer will work on the station for a set number of repetitions or a set time before moving on to the next station.

6. You can vary how hard a performer works by adjusting:
   - the length of time on each station/number of repetitions at each station
   - the number of times the performer must complete the circuit within one training session
   - the number of times the performer must complete the circuit training session per week
   - the amount of recovery time you allow between each station/complete circuit.

Circuit training can be used to improve any component of fitness (including skill aspects related to a specific sporting activity), as the exercises and the order in which they are completed can be adapted to suit many needs. For example, as a form of continuous exercise circuit training can improve cardiovascular endurance. By working on specific groups of muscles at several stations, it can also increase muscular endurance. Strength could also be worked on by including

QUESTION

Which principle of training is being applied by increasing the intensity of the exercise? Match each of the bullet points (left) to the FITT principle (see Chapter 4). Which principle of training are you considering if you only increase the intensity gradually?

weight-bearing exercises (such as press-ups, tricep dips and bench presses using a bench to add resistance), and skills such as passing, shooting, dribbling can be included to improve relevant skill-related aspects of fitness such as agility and coordination.

Straight dribble	Press-up	Skipping
Chest pass (against the wall)	Sit-up	Tricep dip
Zigzag dribble	Shuttle run	Bench astride
Shooting		

Table 5.4 Activities of circuit training

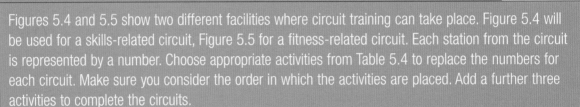

ACTION

Figures 5.4 and 5.5 show two different facilities where circuit training can take place. Figure 5.4 will be used for a skills-related circuit, Figure 5.5 for a fitness-related circuit. Each station from the circuit is represented by a number. Choose appropriate activities from Table 5.4 to replace the numbers for each circuit. Make sure you consider the order in which the activities are placed. Add a further three activities to complete the circuits.

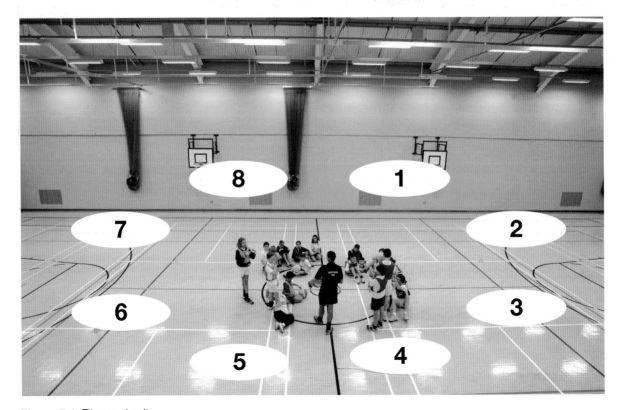

Figure 5.4 Fitness circuit

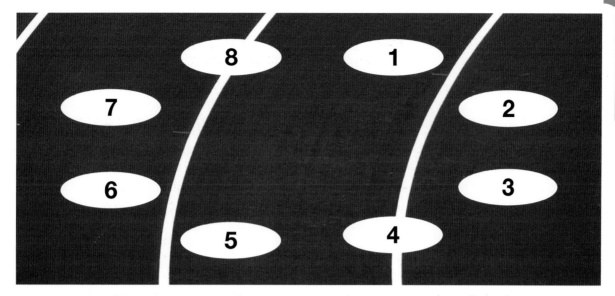

Figure 5.5 Skills circuit

Fartlek training

This is another form of continuous training. It involves running at different paces and over different terrains. For example, rather than road-running at a constant pace, you might increase your speed for 50 metres and then jog until you have sufficiently recovered before sprinting again. You could run 'off road' through woodland, changing your pace as you go up and down hill. It is a very good training method for games players as it can be tailored to match the demands of the game, ie mixing spells of relative inactivity (jogging) with intense activity (sprinting).

Cross training

Cross training combines two or more different types of exercise. Performers whose activities demand a wide range of fitness may use this training method, eg tri-athletes or decathletes. A tri-athlete may run in one training session, swim in another, cycle during the third and lift weights in their fourth training session, all within one week. This type of training allows the performer to train all of the required areas of fitness for their activity.

HOMEWORK

In the previous action, the fitness and skill circuits were kept separate, but they can be combined. Choose a team game and design a suitable circuit for someone who plays that game. Make sure you include activities relevant to the game and to the components of fitness you think are important to that game. Explain your choice of activities within your circuit to others in your class.

Interval training

Interval training is a form of intermittent training. Breaks are built into the training session in order to allow the performer to recover, so that they can continue to work at high levels of intensity. The 'interval' is the period when they reduce the amount of work they are doing to allow recovery.

Due to the use of intervals, this type of training is normally considered for high-intensity work. Sprinters, swimmers and cyclists typically use this type of training, although it can be adapted to suit almost any activity by altering the duration of the work interval, how hard the performer works in the work interval, the number of repetitions within a set, the number of sets, the length of the rest interval and the type of activity carried out during the rest.

Figure 5.6 gives an example of an interval training session.

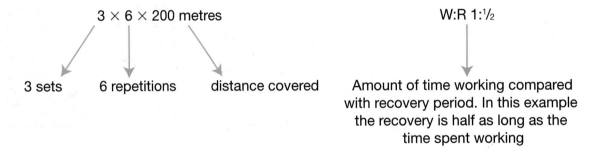

Figure 5.6 Example of interval training session

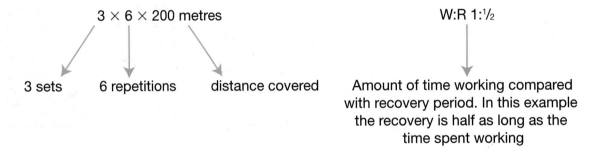

QUESTION

Would the following interval training sessions be for a performer preparing for an aerobic or anaerobic activity?

- $5 \times 10 \times 50$ metres   W:R 1:3   Aerobic/anaerobic?
- $5 \times 1 \times 3000$ metres W:R 1:½ Aerobic/anaerobic?

Weight training

Weight training is a form of strength training. You can use free weights (weights that are not attached to machines, eg dumb bells) or weights that are part of a gym machine.

You can train to improve muscular strength or muscular endurance. If you chose to increase muscular endurance you would need to lift the weights repeatedly for a number of repetitions and a number of sets. The general standard is between 12 to 20 repetitions per set, for three sets. The

Figure 5.7 Free weights

Figure 5.8 Machine-based weights

weight you use should be light enough to allow you to complete the sets. Strength training, however, requires fewer repetitions and sets but heavier weights. Performers requiring power (eg sprinters and field athletes competing in throwing events) would design their weight training so that they increased their strength, whereas performers who rely heavily on muscular endurance (eg middle- to long-distance runners and racket players) would design their programme to increase their muscular endurance.

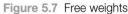

ACTION

Match the images in Figure 5.9 (p. 44) to the training methods discussed.

? QUESTION

Now that you have read about each of the relevant training methods, which ones do you think are continuous and which ones are interval? Can any be adapted to become either continuous or interval?

? QUESTION

Which training method would be most appropriate to you given your activity, your role within it and your individual needs?

Figure 5.9

QUESTION

What type of training could you do at the locations in Figure 5.10?

Figure 5.10

Figure 5.11

ACTION

Match the performers in Figure 5.11 to the most relevant training method (exam hint – go for the most obvious answers).

ACTION

Tick each training method in Table 5.5 which you could use to improve each of the components of fitness listed.

	Continuous	Fartlek	Circuit	Interval	Weight
Flexibility					
Muscular endurance					
Muscular strength					
Body composition					
Cardio-vascular endurance					
Power					
Agility					
Speed					

Table 5.5 Matching training methods with components of fitness

Target zones

It is important to train at the correct intensity for your activity (aerobic or anaerobic) and for yourself (considering your age and current level of fitness). To help us achieve the correct training intensity we can use target training zones.

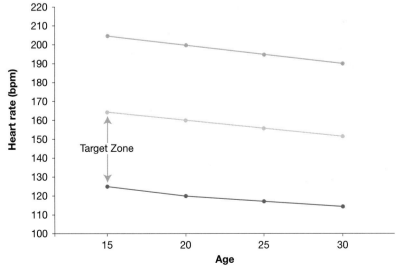

Figure 5.12 Thresholds of training and target zones

? QUESTION

Use the graph in Figure 5.12 to give the target zone heart rates for the following:

- a club swimmer aged 25
- a school tennis player aged 15
- a veteran rugby player aged 30.

The top line on the graph in Figure 5.12 represents the maximum heart rate (beats per minute – bpm) values for the age groups specified (15, 20, 25, 30). This value is calculated by taking the performer's age from the base rate of 220 bpm. The middle line represents the maximum training threshold (80 per cent of maximum heart rate) and the lower line represents the minimum training threshold (60 per cent of maximum heart rate). The area between the minimum and maximum training thresholds is called the **target zone**, ie it is the area that you should try to work within so that your body is working hard enough to cause it to adapt, but not so hard that the training has a negative effect.

What happens to the target zone as the performer gets older?

? QUESTION

What happens to the target zone as the performer gets older?

? QUESTION

Table 5.6 shows the actual heart rate values used to produce the graph in Figure 5.12.

If maximum heart rate is calculated by subtracting the performer's age from 220, enter the heart rate values for performers aged 45 and 50 and their target zones.

	15	20	25	30	35	40	45	50
Max heart rate (MHR)	205	200	195	190	185	180		
80% MHR	164	160	156	152	148	144		
60% MHR	123	120	117	114	111	108		

Table 5.6 Calculating heart rate values

The effects of exercise

The purpose of training is to become fitter so that the body is able to cope more easily with the physical demands placed upon it. The reason that the body is more able to cope is because it adapts to the training. Your body changes as a result of physical work, and these changes are summarised below. You are not expected to know all of these changes, but it is a good idea to learn at least two of each of the adaptations. Exam questions will ask about the immediate effects of exercise, the effects of regular training and the long-term benefits of exercise to the body. It is important that you know the difference between these terms.

Immediate effects

As soon as you take part in physical activity your body experiences some **immediate** effects. These are changes that take place on a temporary basis straight away to give immediate help, so that you can complete the work you are asking of your body. There will be changes to heart rate, breathing rate and body temperature, for example. Heart rate increases to speed up oxygen delivery to the muscles, while the breathing rate increases to take in more air containing oxygen and to remove increased levels of carbon dioxide. Once exercise has stopped you body will *slowly* return back to its pre-exercise state in terms of heart rate, breathing rate and body temperature.

Effects of regular training

If you continue to exercise on a regular basis, following the principles of training, your body will start to adapt to its increased workload, so that in effect the work becomes easier for the body to do (in other words, you become fitter). These adaptations are what you should refer to if asked about the **effects** of regular training. For example, if the heart has been working harder on a regular basis it becomes used to this, and over time increases its strength so that it is easier for it to pump a larger amount of blood out of the heart per beat. When this happens we say that the performer has an **increased stroke volume** (see Chapter 9). This is a benefit of regular training: the performer will have a larger stroke volume even when they are at rest (because while still training on a regular basis the heart will *maintain* its new level of strength), and as a result the performer's heart rate at rest will be lower (see Chapter 9).

Long-term benefits of exercise

Changes to the body as a result of regular exercise can also bring about **long-term** benefits of exercise; eg exercise can bring about a drop in blood pressure. High blood pressure is a common health risk as people grow older. If blood pressure is too high, it can lead to coronary heart failure or a stroke (as the blood is not able to circulate through the blood vessels properly). A long-term benefit of exercise is therefore that blood pressure can be reduced, reducing some of the risk factors that cause coronary heart disease and strokes.

ACTION

Take part in physical activity for a couple of minutes (eg skipping, jumping, running up and down stairs), or think back to the last time you had a practical session. What were the immediate effects of exercise that you noticed? Can you think of an immediate effect to record in each of the spaces in Table 5.7? (Some possible answers are given in Table 5.9 at the end of the chapter.)

	Immediate effect of exercise
Muscles	
Cardiovascular system	
Respiratory system	

Table 5.7 Immediate effects of exercise

When asked a question on this aspect of the course, make sure you double-check whether you are being asked about:

- the immediate effects of exercise
- the effects of regular training, or
- the long-term benefits of exercise.

	Effects of regular training (aerobic or anaerobic)	Long-term benefits of exercise
Bones	Increased strength	Reduction in risk of osteoporosis
Muscles	Muscle hypertrophy Increased mitochondria Increased myoglobin	Increased strength
Cardiovascular system	Cardiac hypertrophy Increased stroke volume Drop in resting heart rate Increased cardiac output during exercise Increased capillarisation Increase in red blood cells	Drop in resting blood pressure Reduction in coronary heart disease risk factors
Respiratory system	Drop in resting respiratory rate Increased strength in respiratory muscles Increased efficiency of exchange of gases at the alveoli Increased surface area of alveoli Slight increase in vital capacity Slight increase in tidal volume	Increased efficiency resulting in increase in aerobic work

Table 5.8 Effects of exercise on the body

Obviously these three areas are linked. We experience the immediate effects of exercise, which if brought into play on a regular basis (through regular exercise) become permanent adaptations (while the level of activity is maintained). These adaptations then bring health benefits. A summary of the regular effects of training and long-term benefits of exercise are given in Table 5.8.

Recovery rates

One of the immediate effects of exercise is an increase in heart rate. A person's recovery rate is the amount of time it takes for their heart rate to return back to its resting rate after they have finished exercising. The reason the heart rate remains high is that it is continuing to deliver an increased amount of oxygen to the muscles (this is called paying back the **oxygen debt**), to reduce lactic acid content and to transport carbon dioxide to the lungs. The quicker your heart rate returns to its resting value the fitter you are thought to be.

ACTION

Take your resting heart rate and plot it on the graph in Figure 5.13. Take part in some aerobic exercise for five minutes. At the end of the exercise, take your heart rate again and plot on the graph. Continue to take your heart rate every minute until it is back to your resting level. Compare your heart rate values with others' in your group. Whose heart rate returned to resting the quickest? Does this mean that that person is the fittest, or is there another reason for the differences in heart rate?

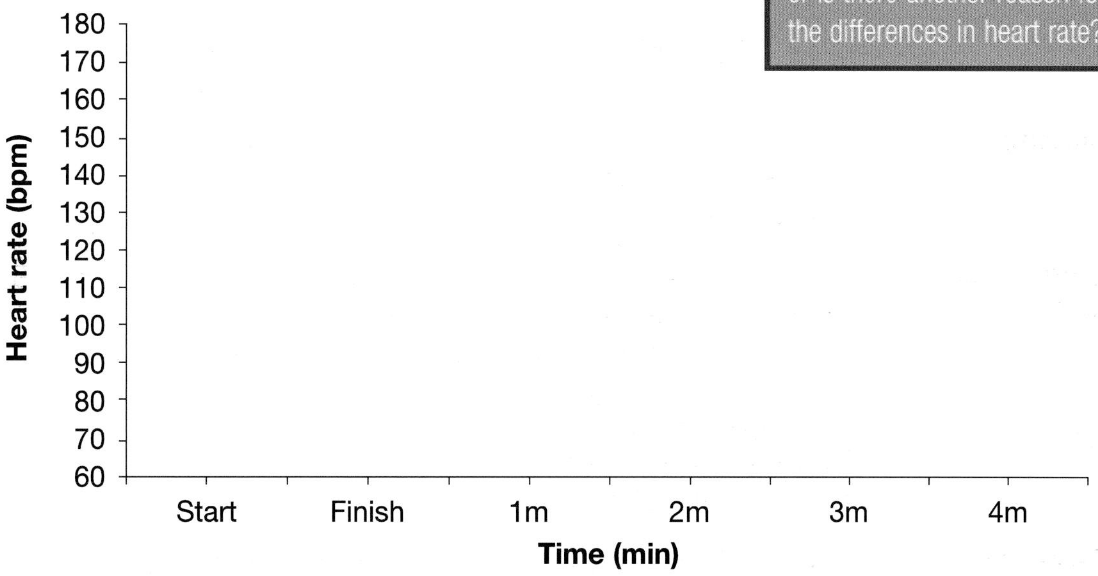

Figure 5.13 Graph showing heart rate values in bpm

Considerations for your PEP

You should use your PEP to demonstrate your understanding of the work you have completed so far. You should consider the following:

- the requirements of the activity (specificity – aerobic? anaerobic?)
- your goal/aim (areas of fitness to improve – individual

HOMEWORK

Fill in the boxes in Figure 5.14 to explain an immediate effect of exercise and a long-term benefit of training on the system indicated in the boxes.

differences) – do not forget this can be to increase fitness after injury (ie as part of a rehabilitation programme)

- which training method will help you achieve your goal/aim
- how you can apply overload
- the rate at which you want to apply overload (progression)
- the structure of the exercise session (warm up, main activity, cool down)
- the possible use of target zones to set training levels
- the possible use of recovery rates to monitor progress.

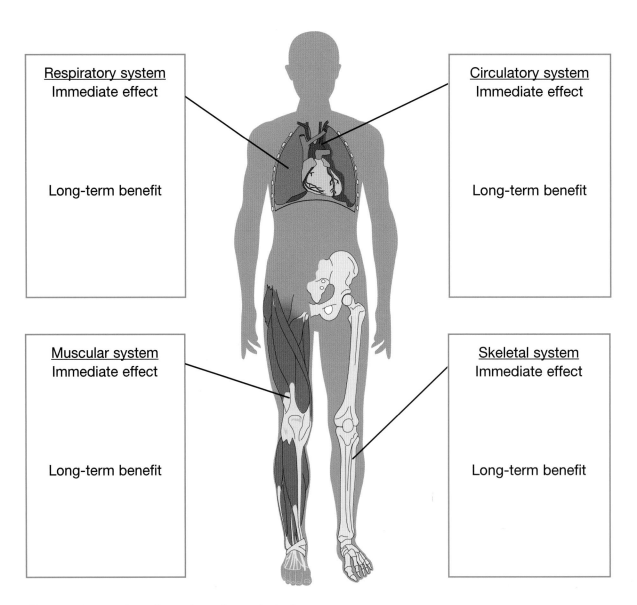

Respiratory system
Immediate effect

Long-term benefit

Circulatory system
Immediate effect

Long-term benefit

Muscular system
Immediate effect

Long-term benefit

Skeletal system
Immediate effect

Long-term benefit

Figure 5.14 Immediate effects of exercise on the body

	Immediate effects of exercise
Muscles	Increased carbon dioxide production Muscle fatigue due to increased acidity in muscle cells and blood
Cardiovascular system	Increase in heart rate and cardiac output, redistribution of blood flow
Respiratory system	Increased breathing rate

Table 5.9 Possible answers to Table 5.7

chapter six
DIET, HEALTH AND HYGIENE

GOALS

By the end of this section you should be able to:

☐ state the requirements of a balanced diet and the role played by each of the components

☐ explain how sporting activity can affect nutritional requirements

☐ state the variables affecting optimum weight

☐ state and describe the extreme categories of somatotyping and link each extreme body type to physical activity

☐ explain the effects of socially acceptable and unacceptable drugs on health and performance

☐ explain the potential dangers of drug use in sport

☐ explain the need for personal hygiene

☐ describe the conditions of a verruca and athlete's foot and their respective treatments.

A balanced diet

It is very important to eat a balanced diet, whether or not you take part in physical activity. The word **diet** refers to what you eat, although it is often used to suggest that someone needs to change his or her eating habits. You have probably heard other people say that they need to 'go on a diet', or make reference to specific diets such as low-fat or low-carbohydrate diets. 'Diet' in all of these cases is being used in a slightly different way. For the purposes of this course you need to think of diet as what you eat, and a balanced diet as what you *should* eat.

A balanced diet is important as it will give you all of the nutrients you need to help you keep healthy and to provide the right amount of energy for the physical work that you do.

Current health studies show that a healthy balanced diet should contain:

- carbohydrates (starchy foods such as bread, potatoes, rice and pasta)
- fats (dairy products, fatty meat, sweets)
- protein (found in meat, fish, eggs and beans)
- vitamins (mainly from fresh fruit and vegetables)
- minerals (found in most foods, particularly vegetables)
- water (found in most food and obviously liquids)
- fibre (found in vegetables, fruits, nuts, cereal).

Most people will eat a mixture of foods from these groups but not necessarily in the correct proportions. Figure 6.1 shows the suggested ratio of these groups to achieve a balanced diet. (Water has not been included as it is not actually a food group.)

QUESTION

Why is it acceptable for some people to eat more than others?

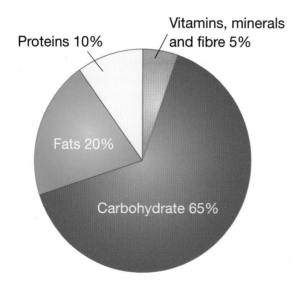

Figure 6.1 Representation of food groups in a balanced diet

Different texts will show slightly different percentages, but it is important to see from the different available sources of information that:

- all food groups are represented
- carbohydrates make up the bulk of our diet
- fats should not be removed from the diet completely.

? QUESTION

Can you remember the difference between aerobic and anaerobic activity? Explain it to a partner and ask them to give you an example of each activity type.

Why do we need these food groups?

Carbohydrates are used to provide the body with energy for physical work. They can be used during aerobic or anaerobic activity.

Fats are used to provide the body with energy for physical work and to keep the body warm. They are used in aerobic activity.

Protein is generally used for growth and repair of new cells within the body, but can be used as an energy source in extreme circumstances (in other words, when usual energy sources are depleted). Protein is obviously very important to a sports performer as it is used in **muscular hypertrophy** (an effect of regular training, where the muscle increases in size).

Vitamins and minerals are necessary because they help in the formation of the tissues of our body, eg hair, skin, nails, teeth and bones. They are also used in chemical reactions in the body.

Fibre is an essential aid to digestion. It is not digested by the body, but slowly makes its way through our digestive system before being expelled with other unwanted substances.

Water is essential in our diet, although it is not a food group. It prevents us from becoming dehydrated and helps to regulate body temperature. During periods of exercise we should make sure we drink more water than we do at rest to replace the water lost through sweating.

ACTION

Match the images in Figure 6.2 to the correct food group in Table 6.1 by ticking the appropriate box (remember, many foods contain more than one food group).

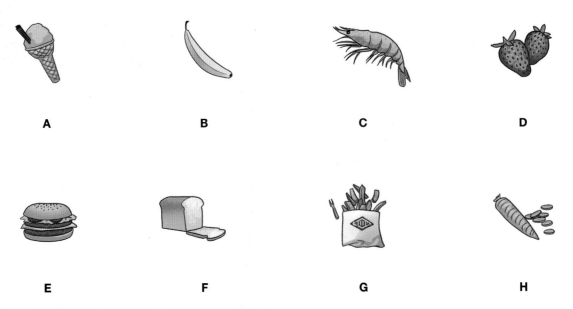

Figure 6.2 Match the foods shown to the correct food group

Image: Food Group ⇩	A	B	C	D	E	F	G	H
Fats								
Carbohydrates								
Proteins								
Minerals								
Vitamins								
Water								
Fibre								

Table 6.1 Foods and food groups

How can sporting activity affect nutritional requirements?

The more physical work we do, the more energy we need to complete it. Food contains **calories**, which are used within the body to release energy for physical work. Sports performers will use more calories than those who do not exercise, and so can afford to consume more food for energy. Performers must be careful, however, that they do not eat too much, otherwise excess carbohydrates will be stored as fat and provide additional weight. This will mean that they have to work harder every time they exercise because of the extra weight they are carrying. Athletes must ensure that Energy IN = Energy OUT.

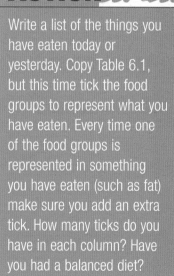

ACTION

Write a list of the things you have eaten today or yesterday. Copy Table 6.1, but this time tick the food groups to represent what you have eaten. Every time one of the food groups is represented in something you have eaten (such as fat) make sure you add an extra tick. How many ticks do you have in each column? Have you had a balanced diet?

? QUESTION

1. If we eat more calories than we use, what do you think the outcome will be?

2. If we eat fewer calories than we need, what do you think the outcome will be?

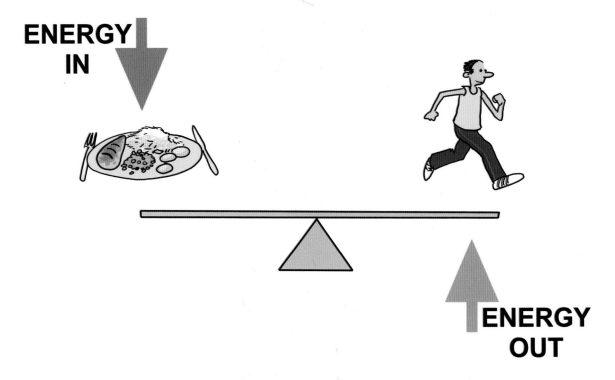

Figure 6.3 The energy equation

Variables affecting optimum weight

Guidelines are given by government health departments about people's optimum weight (the best weight for you). These charts suggest whether someone is overweight or not by considering age, height and gender. It is important to remember that these are only guidelines as optimum weight varies between individuals depending on the following factors.

Sex

There are differences in the structure and physiology of men's and women's bodies (you probably knew that!). On average, men have more muscle mass than women, although there are always exceptions. So even if a man and a woman were the same height, you would expect the man to weigh more than the woman due to the increased weight of their muscle. Because of this, men have an advantage over women in strength events, which is one of the reasons why men and women do not normally compete against each other in activities relying heavily on strength.

Height

The taller you are, the more you would be expected to weigh, therefore in some events it is helpful to be short because you will weigh less. For example, jockeys are normally very small and try to keep their weight as low as possible. Why do you think they need to do this?

Bone structure

Bone also weighs heavily. Some people have a bigger bone structure than others and so will weigh more. This could be an advantage in contact sports where bone strength is important to withstand physical contact.

Muscle girth

This is the size or circumference of the muscle. A larger circumference implies larger muscles, which explains why someone with large muscles may weigh more than the expected standard.

Being the 'correct weight' is important in most sports, but particularly important in the following activities. Do you known why?

- horse racing
- gymnastics
- boxing

Elite sports performers pay a lot of attention to their diet to make sure it is correct for their activity. The performers listed in Table 6.2 (page 60) are all clearly the correct weight for their activities, but how does their weight compare with the 'expected' weight for their age and height using standard tables?

ACTION

Look at the information in Table 6.2 on page 60.

- Which performer is the shortest? What activity do they participate in?
- Consider the approximate weight and guideline weight for each of the performers. What do you notice? If the weight is more than that recommended, what might be causing the extra weight? If the weight is under that expected, why might this be the case?
- Can you see any link between weight and activity? Why are these performers considered to be the correct weight for what they do?
- What does this tell you about using standardised tables to judge whether you are overweight or underweight?

Performer	M/F	Activity	Height (cm)	Guideline weight (kg) based on age and height	Approximate weight (kg)
Franki Detorri	M	Jockey	162.6	59	53
Paula Radcliffe	F	Long distance runner	172.7	63.5	54
David Beckham	M	Football	182.9	80.7	75.7
Jonah Lomu	M	Rugby	195.6	94.3	125
Martin Johnson	M	Rugby	200.7	99.8	119

Table 6.2 Comparing guidelines with sport requirements

Overweight

This is a term used to describe people who 'have weight in excess of normal'. This judgement is based on expected weight for people's height, age and sex. This excess weight may be caused by fat, but it could also be due to muscle, bone and/or water content of the body; eg a bodybuilder with limited fat content could still be overweight, due to the amount of muscle they have.

Underweight

Underweight is a term used to describe people who do not have the recommended amount of body fat in relation to their age and height.

Overfat

This term is:

a way of saying that you have more body fat than you should have.

Obese

Obese is:

a term used to describe people who are very overfat.

It refers to the person having an abnormally high proportion of body fat in their bodies. This is a potentially harmful condition due to the additional strain it places on the body's systems.

Carbohydrates are the main source of [   ]

for a performer, but they may also gain energy from

[   ] and [   ] . [   ] are

also used for growth and repair of tissue so play an

important role if the performer has suffered an

[   ] . Dehydration results if insufficient

[   ] is consumed before, during or after an

activity. Fibre is important in maintaining healthy

[   ] movement. [   ] and

[   ] are the remaining components of a

balanced diet, they are essential to the help in the

formation of [   ] and for [   ]

reactions in the body.

Figure 6.4

ACTION

Complete the statements in Figure 6.4 about diet.

ACTION

Find some images of elite track athletes (newspapers or the internet are potentially good sources). Make a collage of the athletes to display on the wall. Look at their body composition. You should notice that it is difficult to see any additional fat stores under their skin regardless of whether they are a sprinter, middle-distance or long-distance runner. These athletes are achieving the correct energy balance for their events. Do all elite track and field athletes have the same physique? If not, why do you think this is?

Somatotyping

William Sheldon described three general body types. He called them:

- ectomorph
- mesomorph
- endomorph.

Ectomorphs

Ectomorphs are considered to have the following characteristics:

- tall and thin (skeletal height is the most important measurement)
- delicate build
- lightly muscled
- suitable body type for endurance activities.

Mesomorphs

Mesomorphs' characteristics are:

- muscular or athletic build (width of the shoulders is the most important measurement)
- gain muscle relatively easily
- add little fat
- built for physical activity involving speed and/or strength and/or power.

Endomorphs

The characteristics of endomorphs are:

- larger individuals with a rounded appearance (the width of the hips is the most important measurement)
- have trouble losing weight
- can gain muscle
- only suited to specific sports that do not require speed or mobility due to additional weight.

These general body types are extreme, ie very few people are completely endomorph, mesomorph or ectomorph.

Ectomorph	Mesomorph	Endomorph
Narrow shoulders and Narrow hips	Wide shoulders and Narrow hips	Wide hips and Narrow shoulders

Table 6.3 Classic shapes

HOMEWORK

Find as many pictures of **elite** performers from as many different sporting events as you can, and combine them with someone else's from your group. Organise the images into groups based on the body types of the performers, not by activity.

- Do any of the groups of images fall into Sheldon's three categories?
- If so, which categories are represented?
- Even though you did not sort the images on sporting activity, do the images within each group tend to be from the same type of activity anyway?
- What does this tell you about the required body type for that activity?
- Are any of Sheldon's body types not represented? What does this tell you about the suitability of that body type for physical activity?

The effects of smoking and alcohol on health and performance

Smoking

There is growing pressure on governments to ban smoking in public places. Bans are already in existence in many states within the USA, and partial bans operate in the UK. The desire for these bans is based on growing evidence that passive smoking as well as active smoking is harmful to our health, leading to heart and lung disease, cancer and premature death.

- If you smoke, you are two to three times more likely to have a heart attack than a non-smoker, and much more likely to die from heart disease. Smokers are also more likely to have strokes, blood clots, and angina.

- Tobacco smoking can result in respiratory diseases like emphysema and chronic bronchitis, and leaves sufferers breathless and unable to do much activity.

- As a smoker, your risk of developing diabetes in adult life is two to three times higher than that of a non-smoker.

- Tobacco contains nicotine, which is addictive. This is why giving up smoking is so difficult, even though people know the risks of continuing.

Apart from the obvious health risks, smoking will decrease performance in practical activity due to the carbon monoxide contained in cigarette smoke. The **haemoglobin** in the red blood cells that is normally used to carry oxygen will carry carbon monoxide in preference, reducing the amount of oxygen available to release energy and the performer's ability to work aerobically. Heavy smokers may have as much as ten per cent of their haemoglobin bound by carbon monoxide. This obviously has more of an effect on performers in endurance events, but will affect the recovery of all performers. (How many elite 100 metre sprinters do you see smoking?)

Alcohol

Many people drink moderate amounts of alcohol to be sociable. The immediate effects of alcohol vary depending on the amount consumed, and therefore the amount of alcohol in the blood. If low amounts of alcohol are consumed you can witness the following effects:

- relaxes the drinker
- reduces tension
- lowers inhibitions
- impairs concentration
- slows reflexes
- impairs reaction time
- reduces coordination
- causes loss of balance.

While the first two bullet points might release stress, the last five points will have a negative impact on performance. As a result, alcohol should not be drunk before sporting activity. Like nicotine, alcohol can become addictive.

Long-term effects of drinking too much alcohol include:

- increased weight (due to the calories in alcohol)
- cancer of the liver and/or bowel
- heart failure
- high blood pressure.

ACTION

Choose a sporting activity and complete Table 6.4 by giving an example of how the stated effects of alcohol would affect a performer in the activity you have chosen.

Effect of alcohol	Example of how performance is affected
Impairs concentration	
Slows reflexes	
Impairs reaction time	
Reduces co-ordination	
Loss of balance	
Increased weight	

Table 6.4 Effects of alcohol on physical activity

Performance-enhancing drugs

Elite performers dedicate their lives to becoming as good as they can possibly be, and hopefully the best in their chosen activity. They are under huge amounts of pressure to find ways to increase their performance, and for some the pressure is so great that they turn to performance-enhancing drugs – ie drugs that will help them perform to an even higher standard in their sport.

The problem with this is that the use of performance-enhancing drugs is banned and considered to be cheating, so anyone found taking drugs would be disqualified. The two main reasons they are banned are:

1. they artificially improve your performance, so if you take them you are cheating
2. taking the drugs may improve performance, but they also present dangerous side effects, which the athletes should be protected from.

Table 6.5 (page 66) summarises the drugs you should be aware of, the advantages to the performer and some of their harmful side effects. You will not be exepcted to know actual examples of drugs, but you do need to know the type (class) of drug, why performers might take them and the potentially damaging side effects.

QUESTION ?

Why do you think elite athletes are under so much pressure to find ways to improve their performance?

Drug type/ class	Examples	Possible ways to enhance performance	Example of harmful side effects
Stimulants	Amphetamines Caffeine	Increase in physical/mental alertness Increased confidence Increased metabolic rate	Aggression Anxiety Insomnia Irregular and increased heart rate
Narcotic analgesics	Methadone Morphine Codeine	Reduce pain felt, therefore 'hides' injury	Nausea and vomiting Loss of concentration Loss of balance/ coordination May lead to permanent injury Addiction
Anabolic steroids	Testosterone Nandrolone	Train harder for longer, therefore increase strength/power	Liver/kidney damage Aggression Premature heart disease Acne Low sperm count
Diuretics	Bendrofluazide	Quick weight loss, therefore can 'make weight' for specific weight category Urine passed sooner, therefore if other drugs taken 'evidence' is passed out of the body sooner	Dehydration Nausea Kidney/liver failure
Beta blockers	Atenolol Propranolol	Calm and relaxing effect	Tiredness Low blood pressure
Blood doping*	OR use of EPO (erythopoietin)	Increases red blood cell count, therefore increases the oxygen-carrying capacity of the blood	Increased viscosity (thickness/stickiness) therefore increased risk of heart failure

* Although not a drug, this practice is banned as it is still used to enhance performance and has dangerous side effects

Table 6.5 Effects of drugs on the body

ACTION

Research the most recent major sporting championships (eg, Athens 2004 Olympic Games, the European Indoor Athletics Championships, or the World Weight Lifting Championships). Try to find further examples of reports of performers who have failed drugs tests and therefore are accused of taking performance-enhancing drugs. Add their details to Table 6.6. Consider the performers in column 1, their sport and the drug they were accused of taking; complete column 4 by giving an example of a way in which their performance may benefit by taking this drug, then complete column 5 by giving a harmful side effect that they may experience as a result.

Performer 1	Sporting Activity 2	Drug accused of taking 3	How would it improve their performance? 4	Possible harmful side effects of this type of drug 5
Ben Johnson	Sprinting	Steroids		
Jan Ullrich	Cycling	Amphetamine		
Johann Muehlegg	Cross-country skiing	Steroids		
Diego Maradona	Football	Stimulants		
Frankie Dettori	Horse racing	Diuretics		

Table 6.6 Performers who have failed drugs tests

ACTION

Complete the word search on the handout provided by your teacher to find the names of performance-enhancing drugs AND some possible side effects. The words you are looking for are given in Table 6.7.

Stimulants	Painkiller	Train
Stimulate	Beta blockers	Diuretics
Longer	CNS	Alert
Blood doping	Increase oxygen	Harder

Table 6.7 Drugs and their side effects

PERFORMANCE-ENHANCING DRUGS WORD SEARCH

S	A	D	V	U	Q	U	J	A	E	T	O	C	O	G
G	R	L	K	R	D	P	W	R	L	J	Q	W	O	N
W	U	E	E	R	J	I	Z	E	Y	X	W	K	C	I
K	R	J	K	R	O	C	U	D	T	R	A	I	N	P
H	R	X	Z	C	T	Y	X	R	T	M	S	O	S	O
N	E	G	Y	X	O	E	S	A	E	R	C	N	I	D
U	D	B	D	E	L	L	Y	H	E	T	C	P	J	D
U	U	W	T	V	S	P	B	L	J	V	I	I	Z	O
S	C	S	T	I	M	U	L	A	N	T	S	C	R	O
E	T	A	L	U	M	I	T	S	T	Q	U	E	S	L
C	I	U	E	C	K	S	U	H	Z	E	G	M	O	B
S	O	F	G	N	F	D	Z	V	G	N	B	X	P	Z
B	N	Y	I	T	G	O	W	B	O	I	H	P	J	V
K	E	A	E	F	G	C	G	L	O	Q	E	S	G	G
S	P	N	G	J	C	E	S	Z	T	Y	N	W	M	N

ACTION

Use the words you find in the word search (or Table 6.7) to complete Table 6.8 by matching the drug type with its effects.

Drug Type	How it enhances performance
	Reduction in central nervous system activity
	Weight loss/mask the presence of other drugs
Anabolic Steroids	
Narcotic Analgesics	

Table 6.8 How drugs can enhance performance

Add an extra column to Table 6.8, giving an example of a sporting activity often associated with the illegal drug, due to the way the drug may enhance performance.

Hygiene

To complete this chapter on general health, we need to consider briefly personal hygiene and two minor skin infections.

Obviously we all need to maintain high standards of personal hygiene, if for no other reason than to be considerate to those around us. This should involve washing regularly (our bodies and our clothing). This becomes even more important after physical activity, as we become hot when we exercise. In order to cool us down our bodies sweat; if we do not wash this away then bacteria on the skin feed on the sweat, producing an unpleasant odour.

Common skin infections include **verrucas** and **athlete's foot**, which can spread easily. You should be aware of their signs and symptoms so that you can treat them and also take precautions so that you reduce the chance of passing them on to others.

A **verruca** is a virus (V for virus); it looks like a small black dot on the sole of the foot. There are several products at the chemist that can be used to remove the verruca slowly. These products are normally 'painted' onto the verruca and left to work.

Athlete's foot is a fungus and often appears as flaky, itchy skin between the toes. It is treated by using medicated powder which is dusted on to the infected area.

DIET, HEALTH AND HYGIENE

Across:

4 Smoking is a socially _____ drug in some areas.

7 Performers who run in long distance events normally have this body type.

9 Which word is being defined? 'A way of saying you have more body fat than you should have.'

12 Used in aerobic activities for energy.

14 Which word is being defined? 'A term used to describe people who are very overfat.'

15 Jockeys need to be this.

Down:

1 I need to shower after activity because an increase in body temperature causes me to _____.

2 Name a sporting activity that requires performers to have an extreme mesomorph body type.

3 _____ is an example of a socially acceptable drug.

5 What is this? Found on the foot, often between the toes.

6 Causes dehydration.

8 If I eat more calories than I burn I will become _____.

10 If I increase my training I need to eat _____.

11 Used by the body as an energy source.

13 Basketball players are usually this. It helps them reach the basket.

Safety Aspects and Risk Assessment in Physical Activity and Sport

2

chapter seven
PREVENTION OF INJURY

GOALS

By the end of this section you should be able to:

☐ explain the relevance of the following factors in preventing injury:

1. the rules of the game
2. correct clothing; protective clothing; correct equipment
3. balanced competition
4. a warm up

☐ identify the level of risk within a variety of activities.

Taking part in physical activity can be a risky business. According to the US Consumer Product Safety Commission for 1998, the three sports resulting in the most sports injury were rugby, cheerleading and boxing. Look at Figure 7.1 to see some of the potential injuries that can be sustained through taking part in sport.

You would obviously be very unlucky to suffer all of these injuries, but even so you should try to minimise the risk of receiving any injuries.

Why do we need rules?

Rules are in place so that we can all enjoy playing sport. They make the sport fair and encourage good sporting behaviour; they also help to protect us from injury and maintain our safety.

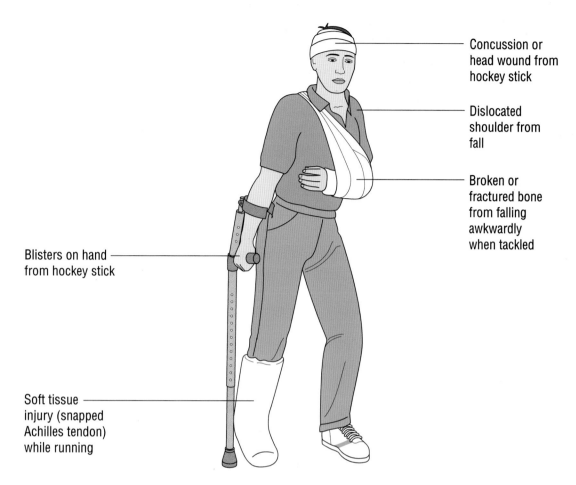

Concussion or head wound from hockey stick

Dislocated shoulder from fall

Broken or fractured bone from falling awkwardly when tackled

Blisters on hand from hockey stick

Soft tissue injury (snapped Achilles tendon) while running

Figure 7.1 Possible sports injuries

Rule	What injury might this protect the players from?
No lifting the stick above head height	
Checking players' studs in their boots before they go onto the pitch	
Taping up or removal of any jewellery	

Table 7.1 Rules to protect players

QUESTION

Look at Table 7.1. How might these rules protect the players?

ACTION

Choose one of the sports for which you will be assessed in your practical. Complete your own table, identifying three rules and how the rule protects the people playing. (Use different examples from those in Table 7.1.)

Clothing and equipment

Rules are not the only way of protecting yourself and others from injury. You need to use the correct

- kit
- protective clothing
- equipment and
- facilities.

Kit

Using the **correct kit** means that your movements will not be restricted by heavy or tight clothing or by clothing that is too baggy or loose (could you play rugby, football or hockey as well with your ordinary clothes on, compared with when you wear your sports kit?). Because your movements are not restricted your level of play should be higher, but you are also less likely to be injured if wearing the correct kit because your footwear will be appropriate for the surface you are playing on (grass, artificial pitch, track, tarmac, gym floor, sports hall; notice how your footwear tends to change as you change the surface you are playing on).

Also, loose clothing could be a problem in sports such as trampolining where it might catch; on the other hand, if clothing is too heavy or tight, you might not be able to perform the correct technique and become injured as a result.

Protective clothing

This is vital in some sports. For example, although the idea in hockey is to stop the ball with your stick, it will hit your shin from time to time. Depending on how hard the ball has been hit, this can be very painful unless you are wearing shin guards. Similarly, players wear mouth guards so that they do not lose their teeth if they are hit with a hockey stick or ball.

Equipment

You should always check the **equipment** you are going to use. Ask yourself, is it safe for use? If the answer is no, do not use it. For example:

- Playing squash or badminton with an inappropriate grip on the handle could lead to the racket flying out of your hand. This might not result in an injury to you, but could mean that a partner or opponent is hit with the racket.

- In basketball, if the hoop is damaged the court should not be used until it is fixed otherwise it could fall and injure those underneath it.

- In netball the goal posts should be checked to make sure the bolts securing the hoops are tight.

The equipment you use may also need some protective clothing! For example:

- Rugby posts have padding around them so that if players run into the posts in the heat of the game, the risk of injury is reduced.

Figure 7.2 Padding around rugby posts

Facilities

The correct **facilities** also need to be used for the sport that you are playing. Sports halls can be used for a variety of activities such as badminton, five-a-side football, netball, volleyball and table tennis, but if there is water on the floor making it slippery, the risk of injury is increased. Activities such as sprinting, however, should not be carried out in a sports hall unless the sprint stops well short of the end wall, or appropriate padding is placed at the end of the wall. Failure to do this would increase the risk of injury as sprinters could hit the end wall at pace, which would

Figure 7.3 Indoor track

probably result in a broken bone. If rugby were played indoors, the rules about tackling would need to change, otherwise the risk of injury when players hit the hard floor would be too great. Other points to consider about facilities include:

- trampolining should only be carried out if the height of the facility allows it
- rugby matches are cancelled if the pitch is frozen
- outdoor netball matches are cancelled if the court is too icy
- long jump pits should always be checked for 'unwanted objects' before use.

ACTION

Work with a partner and think about what issues you should consider regarding facilities for the following activities:

- basketball
- swimming
- discus
- boxing.

Figure 7.4 Long jump pits should be checked before use

Balancing competition

This aspect of sport is also used to help reduce the risk of injury. This means that the competition rules try to make sure that the competition is fair by having evenly matched opposition. This is achieved by making sure that people only compete directly with each other if they are:

- a similar age, or
- the same sex, or
- a similar ability, or
- a similar weight.

ACTION

Name the items of protective clothing in Figure 7.5, the correct sporting activity, and explain how they reduce risk of injury.

ACTION

Look at the pictures in Figure 7.6. List the items of protective clothing, what they are being used to protect and the injury which they are designed to prevent.

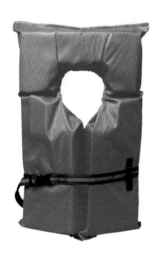

Figure 7.5 Protective clothing

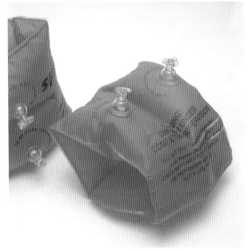

Figure 7.6 What does protective clothing protect?

? QUESTION

How is competition balanced in other activities, eg boxing and badminton?

For example, football competitions will be for different age groups, U12, U13, U14. The U12 side would not play the U21 side. The competition would not be fair because of the size of the U21s compared with the U12s, and their level of skill and experience. Apart from being a poor game because of the inequalities, it would increase the risk of injury to the U12 side. For the same reason, men's and women's football teams do not normally play against each other. The same is true in other sports.

Warm up and cool down

Warm up

A proper **warm up** has many benefits:

- Muscles which are ready for exercise (through completing a warm up) will be able to contract and relax more quickly.
- Oxygen will be more easily available to the muscles because of the increased heat of the body.
- It helps the performer to focus on the task they are about to undertake – it is a psychological preparation.

It will also help reduce the risk of injury: you can ensure that muscles and tendons are ready for action by gently increasing the amount of work they do, rather than just going from static to very active in one step. Therefore, by using a properly planned warm up, the performer is less likely to receive a sprain or strain. A warm up has three phases:

1. Pulse raising/increasing body temperature – this is achieved by completing some form of light continuous activity such as jogging.
2. Stretching, achieved through stretching! You should start from the top and work down, stretching the muscles that will be worked in the main session.
3. Event-specific drills to prepare your body for the activity you are about to do.

Figure 7.7 Warming up

Cool down

Cool downs do not reduce the risk of injury during performance, but they do reduce the risk of muscle stiffness after performance, and speed up the removal of lactic acid (see Chapter 10). They also reduce the risk of fainting after activity by keeping the blood circulating back to the heart and gradually reducing the heart rate (see Chapter 9). Cool downs have two phases:

1. A reduction in body temperature, slow jogging/walking to bring the level of activity down gradually and help removal of carbon dioxide and lactic acid.

2. More stretching to help reduce temperature slowly, to help in the removal of waste products and to stretch the muscles after they have been working to increase the range of movement possible at the joint.

Judging risks in sporting activity

The next activities ask you to judge the risks of various activities. When asked to complete this sort of activity, you should consider the following questions before arriving at a conclusion:

- What would happen if the risk were not prevented? How bad would it be?

Therefore, if offered the choice between archery and badminton, you might decide that archery had the greatest risk as potentially you could do more damage in this activity than badminton. This would be a reasonable conclusion.

- What is the ability/experience of the group taking part in the activity?

If you had a group of beginners white-water rafting, would there be any greater risk than if they were all experienced? You might decide that the inexperienced or beginners group would be at greater risk as they were more likely to get into difficulty, and if they did they would not know how to escape it. Again, this would be a reasonable conclusion. When you cannot tell whether the people are beginners or not, just consider the first question to help you make your judgement.

Sport	Risk (what could happen to you?)	Precaution (how could you help to prevent the risk happening?)
Netball		
White-water rafting		
1500 metres		
Rugby		
Gymnastics		
Climbing		

Table 7.2 Risks and precautions

Figure 7.8 What are the risks?

GOALS

By the end of this section you should be able to:

☐ identify the basic signs and symptoms of the following conditions:

1. fractures

2. joint injuries

3. soft tissue injuries

4. skin damage

5. dehydration

6. hypothermia

7. concussion

8. unconsciousness

☐ explain the following and when they should be applied:

1. DRABC

2. recovery position

3. resuscitation

4. RICE.

It is not the intention of the Edexcel exam board that you should administer first aid or become a first aider. You should always seek medical advice if in any doubt about the seriousness of an injury, but if you are involved in sport, it is important that you can recognise the signs and symptoms of several types of sports injury. You can use this knowledge if you become injured or if immediate action is needed in the case of an emergency. The information that follows is a basic understanding of the conditions and procedures; more detailed information can be obtained from organisations such as St John Ambulance.

Fractures

A fracture is a break or crack in a bone.

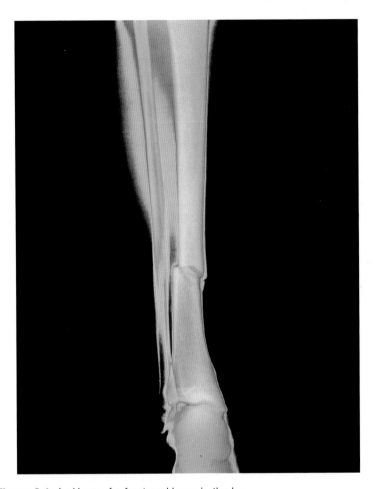

Figure 8.1 An X-ray of a fractured bone in the leg

Fractures occur as a result of direct or indirect force; as a result, they tend to be associated with contact sports. For example, fractures of bones in the lower leg and foot can happen in football as a result of direct force, ie being kicked. An example of an indirect force causing a fracture is when players fall and put their arms out to break their fall. The point of impact is at the wrist/hand, but the force travels along the arm to the shoulder and onto the clavicle (see Chapter 11), which can then fracture.

Symptoms

Symptoms of fractures include:

- difficulty in moving the injured limb
- pain
- distortion of 'natural' shape
- swelling
- bruising.

Joint injuries

There are different types of joint injury that you could be asked questions about.

Dislocation

Dislocations occur at joints, where the bone is moved out of its normal position. Dislocations as a result of sports injuries tend to happen at the shoulder, thumb and finger. They occur as a result of a heavy force acting on the joint; eg diving to score a try in rugby and falling on the shoulder.

Symptoms

These include:

- pain
- distortion of 'natural' shape.

Tennis elbow

This is an injury to the muscles of the forearm that allow you to extend your wrist and turn your palm upward, and the tendon that attaches the muscle to the elbow joint. It is called tennis elbow because the injury is common in tennis – the action of extending your wrist and turning your palm upward is carried out when you play a backhand stroke.

Poor technique or the wrong size of grip on a racket can cause tennis elbow because of the unnecessary force acting on the tissues.

Symptoms

These include:

- pain (on the outside of the arm and elbow)
- stiffness at the elbow joint.

Figure 8.2 Action of hitting the ball can cause tennis elbow

Golfer's elbow

This affects the muscles and tendons responsible for flexing the wrist, and is an injury caused by overuse. The injury is referred to as golfer's elbow because it is associated with that sport.

During a game, golfers need to bend the wrist repeatedly when striking the ball; this can result in golfer's elbow if players play too much. You can develop tennis elbow or golfer's elbow even if you do not play those sports.

Symptoms

These include:

* pain around the elbow joint, normally on the inside of the joint.

Cartilage tear

A torn cartilage at the knee is another joint injury. The cartilage normally fits on the ends of the bones of the knee joint, but if the cartilage is damaged or begins to deteriorate

Figure 8.3 Golfer's elbow can be caused through playing golf

with age, it can tear. The torn piece of cartilage moves in the joint and can become caught or wedged between the bones. If this happens, the knee becomes painful, difficult to move and swollen.

Symptoms

These include:

- pain around the knee joint
- swollen knee
- difficulty in moving.

Twisted ankle

A twisted ankle is also a joint injury, but this is covered in the next section as it is also considered to be a soft tissue injury.

Soft tissue injuries

Bone is made of a hard material, therefore anything that is not bone is called **soft tissue**. This refers to muscles, ligaments and tendons.

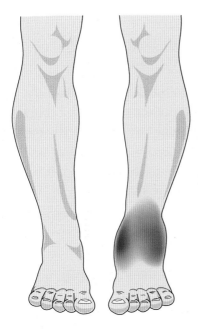

Figure 8.4 Note the bruising and swelling at the ankle as a result of a sprain

Soft tissue injuries are common in sport. In athletics it is not unusual to see an athlete suddenly pull out of a race holding their hamstrings because of a **strained** (torn or pulled) muscle. This usually happens when a muscle is stretched beyond its limits and normally occurs where the tendon joins the muscle.

Other soft tissue injuries include **deep bruising** and **sprains**.

Deep bruising is a bruise of the muscle rather than the skin. Sprains affect ligaments rather than tendons; they occur at or near a joint and are caused by wrenching or twisting of a joint. A twisted ankle is an example of a sprain.

It is often difficult to remember which type of injury is a sprain and which type a strain. You might find it useful to use the '**t**' in strain to remember that it matches the '**t**' in **t**orn or **t**endon.

Symptoms

Strains	Deep bruising	Sprains
• Pain • Visible bruising	• Pain • Swelling • Limited range of movement	• Pain • Swelling • Visible bruising

Table 8.1 Symptoms of soft tissue injuries

Treatment

Soft tissue injuries should be treated using the **RICE** procedure:

- **R Rest** – take a break from the activity. A doctor, nurse or physiotherapist will be able to suggest how long you should rest based on the severity of the injury.
- **I Ice** – apply ice to the injured part (although not directly onto the skin).
- **C Compression** – a bandage is wrapped around the injured part to reduce further swelling and to give support.
- **E Elevation** – lift the injured part. This reduces blood flow to the injury, reducing the amount of bruising.

Skin damage

Players who receive **cuts** that begin to bleed must stop playing immediately to have the cut dressed (covered). Cuts and abrasions or **grazes** are common in sport. Cuts can occur from contact with opponents (eg the studs on their boots), or just another body part (eg a clash of heads). Grazes normally occur if players fall over on harsh surfaces (eg tarmac netball courts, all-weather hockey pitches or frozen fields). A graze takes off the top layers of the skin.

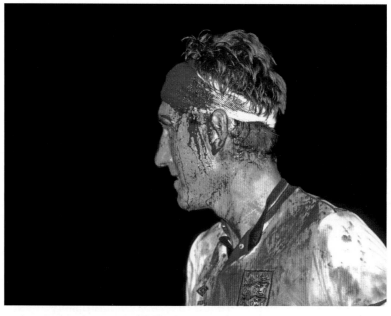

Figure 8.5 A cut on the head should be treated immediately

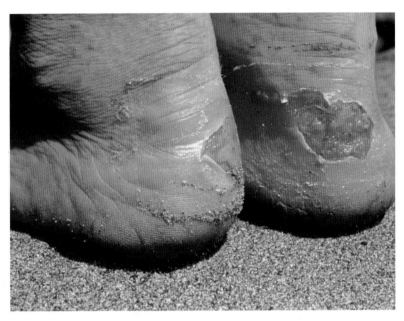

Figure 8.6 Severe blisters on the heels due to ill fitting footwear

Blisters form because of friction. In sport they often occur on the hands because of the rubbing or friction against equipment being held, and on the feet because of the rubbing against the shoes the performer is wearing.

Dehydration

Dehydration occurs when the body has lost too much water and too many minerals. During extreme levels of exercise (or moderate exercise in hot conditions) we can sweat excessively, and unless appropriate water and mineral levels are restored, performers can become dehydrated. This condition tends to affect athletes in endurance events, as they are working for prolonged periods of time. To avoid dehydration, sufficient water must be consumed during the event.

Symptoms

These include:

- thirst
- dry lips
- in severe cases, confusion (sometimes marathon runners are clearly dehydrated by the time they reach the finish line).

Hypothermia

This condition occurs when the body temperature falls below 35°C (normal body temperature is 37°C). Sports performers who perform and train outside in cold temperatures are at risk of this condition; eg climbers, sailors and winter sports enthusiasts. However, any prolonged exposure to the cold could result in hypothermia. To reduce this risk, performers must make sure they warm up properly, wear appropriate clothing to keep them warm, and/or limit the amount of time that they are exposed to the cold.

Symptoms

These include:

- shivering
- pale, cold, dry skin
- lethargy (cannot be bothered to make an effort).

Unconsciousness/concussion

Occasionally, sport performers will receive head injuries; eg two football players jumping to head the ball and clashing heads instead.

Knocking heads hard enough can cause the brain to bounce against the rigid bone of the cranium, which can cause concussion.

Figure 8.7 Two players clashing heads can result in concussion

Symptoms

These include:

- severe headache
- dizziness
- vomiting
- dilation of the pupils
- in more extreme cases, memory loss and blackouts (ie becoming unconscious).

Your treatment of an unconscious or concussed performer will vary depending on whether or not they have a pulse, and whether or not they are breathing.

Emergency treatment

Figure 8.8 includes the following terms:

- DRABC
- recovery position
- mouth-to-mouth ventilation (rescue breaths)
- cardio-pulmonary resuscitation (CPR).

DRABC

This is a useful way of remembering the steps you should take if a sports performer collapses: DR is short for doctor, and A, B, C are easy to remember, as they are the first three letters of the alphabet.

The **D** stands for danger. The idea is that you check the area where the performer is and ask yourself whether or not they are likely to be in more danger if you help them where they are, or if you move them. Usually if someone collapses on a pitch play would stop, but if the event was a cycle race, for example, it might be a good idea to move the cyclist in case others do not see him and run over him.

The **R** stands for response. This is where you find out if the casualty is conscious or not by shaking them (gently) and speaking loudly to them. If there is no response you should assume they are unconscious.

The **A** stands for airway. You should tilt the performer's head back and lift the chin so that the tongue is moved away from the back of the throat, leaving the airway clear for the performer to breath.

B stands for breathing. Once the airway is clear you should

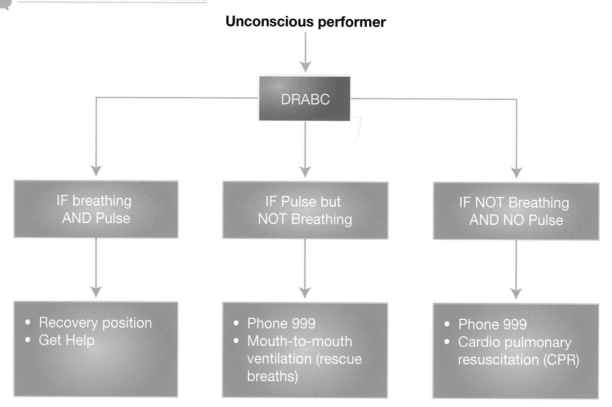

Unconscious performer

DRABC

IF breathing
AND Pulse

IF Pulse but
NOT Breathing

IF NOT Breathing
AND NO Pulse

- Recovery position
- Get Help

- Phone 999
- Mouth-to-mouth
  ventilation (rescue
  breaths)

- Phone 999
- Cardio pulmonary
  resuscitation (CPR)

Figure 8.8 DRABC

check that they *are* breathing by looking for chest movements, hearing them breathe or feeling their breath on your face.

The final check is **C**. This is a check of their circulation – do they have a pulse? You can check this by placing two fingers on the neck, next to the larynx (see Chapter 10). Once you have carried out your assessment, you should be in a position to take the most appropriate action.

Figure 8.9 St John Ambulance recommended recovery position (October 2004)

Recovery position

The reason for placing the performer in the recovery position is that this position stops the tongue from blocking the airway. It allows liquids such as vomit to drain from the mouth so that the performer does not choke on them.

Resuscitation

Mouth-to-mouth ventilation (rescue breaths)

This is ONLY needed when the performer has stopped breathing. The air you exhale still contains oxygen, and so this can be breathed into the performer so that they receive the necessary oxygen to keep them alive. The procedure is as follows:

1. Make sure the airway is open.
2. Pinch the nose to prevent the air that you are breathing into them from coming straight out of the nose.
3. Form a seal around the performer's mouth with your lips (again so the air does not escape), and blow until you see the performer's chest rise.
4. Remove your mouth and watch the chest fall.
5. Repeat and check for circulation (if no circulation, start CPR – see below).
6. If there is circulation, continue to give mouth-to-mouth ventilation for ten more breaths before checking circulation again.

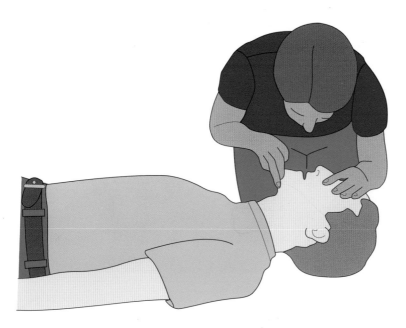

Figure 8.10

7. Carry on until help arrives or the performer begins to breathe.

8. When the performer starts to breathe, STOP and place them in recovery position.

CPR

If there is no pulse, this means that the heart has stopped. The performer's body will therefore have no way of transporting the oxygen being blown into it. CPR is made up of two parts:

- cardiac massage or chest compression
- mouth-to-mouth ventilation (rescue breaths).

The procedure for cardiac massage or chest compression is as follows:

1. Place your hands on the performer's chest, on the lower half of the breast bone, as shown in Figure 8.11.

2. Press down 4–5 cms then release pressure, but keep hands in the same place.

3. Repeat 15 times then give two rescue breaths.

4. Check for circulation if performer's colour improves.

5. If circulation starts, stop cardiac massage but continue with mouth-to-mouth ventilation if necessary. If not necessary, place the casualty in the recovery position.

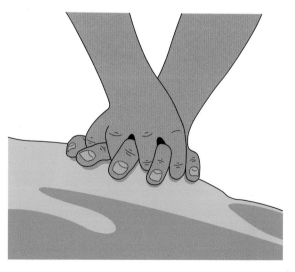

Figure 8.11 Cardiac massage

ACTION

From the information in this chapter you should be able to answer the following true or false questions.

True or false?

1 A performer should be placed in the recovery position if they are breathing and have a pulse.
2 A performer should be placed in the recovery position if they are breathing but do not have a pulse.
3 The recovery position blocks the airways.
4 The R in DRABC stands for resuscitation.
5 Once the performer is breathing, you should stop mouth-to-mouth ventilation.
6 Cardiac massage is used to help restore and maintain the performer's circulation.

ACTION

For each of the sports injuries stated on the cards in Figure 8.15:

- describe a sporting situation that may have lead to this injury
- use your knowledge and understanding of the work covered in the previous chapter to explain how the risk of sustaining the injury could have been reduced.

ACTION

Fill in the blanks. The missing words are all in Table 8.1.

Moving	Head	Footwear	RICE	Bruising
Blisters	Water	Tendon	35	Sprains
DRABC	Inside	Elbow	Deep	Pain
Warm	Spikes	Swelling	Fracture	

Table 8.1 Factors that contribute to sports injuries

A _____ is a break or crack in a bone. Apart from pain, two other symptoms of this injury are _____ and _____.

The pain from golfer's elbow is normally felt on the _____ of the _____ joint.

The pain associated with torn cartilage is due to the cartilage _____ in the joint.

Strains and _____ are soft tissue injuries.

You can strain a muscle or a _____.

Another type of soft tissue injury is _____ bruising.

_____ is a symptom of a soft tissue injury.

All soft tissue injuries should be treated using the _____ procedure.

Grazes occur when players slip on hard surfaces. The risk of this type of injury can be reduced by making sure the player's wear appropriate _____, eg _____ on a running track.

Friction can cause _____ so performers need to make sure that their footwear fits properly.

To reduce the risk of dehydration, endurance performers should make sure they drink plenty of _____ while running.

Hypothermia occurs when the body temperature falls below _____ degrees Celsius. Warming up properly and wearing _____ clothes can reduce the risk of hypothermia.

Concussion is the result of a blow to the _____.

_____ is used to assess a collapsed performer.

ACTION

In teams, number yourselves from one to four. Take it in turns to collect a sports injury card from the front of the class. DO NOT tell anyone else your injury (if you do, you lose the point and the other teams gain one). Think about the symptoms of the injury and mime these to your group. Your group are allowed a maximum of TWO attempts to state the injury based on your mime of the symptoms. If they guess correctly they then have to say what a first aider would do if they came across someone who had that sports injury.

Your team scores one point for correctly guessing the injury and one point for each correct action carried out by the first aider. Once you have had your go, the next team member collects a card.

Some sample cards are shown in Figure 8.15. Create some more in your team and add them to those made by the other teams in your class.

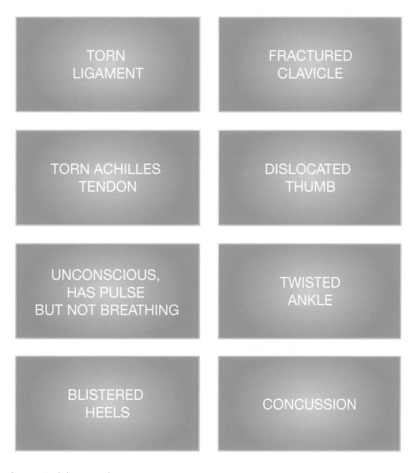

Figure 8.15 Sample sports injury cards

Applied Anatomy and Physiology

3

chapter nine
THE CARDIOVASCULAR SYSTEM (CIRCULATORY SYSTEM)

GOALS

By the end of this section you should be able to:

☐ identify the components of the heart and explain their role

☐ describe the pumping action of the heart

☐ define heart rate, stroke volume and cardiac output and the effects of exercise on them

☐ identify the differences between arteries, capillaries and veins and relate these differences to the role of each vessel type

☐ describe the functions of the components of the blood.

The following five chapters of the book look at the systems within the human body. The reason you need to know about these systems is that they all have a big impact on our ability to take part in sport and on the level of performance we can achieve.

This chapter looks at the cardiovascular system – the **heart**, **blood** and **blood vessels**. The cardiovascular system is vital for sporting performance as it is responsible for:

- transporting increased levels of oxygen (needed to release energy to perform and/or recover from performance) around the body to where it is needed

- regulating our temperature so that we do not overheat during exercise

- removing waste such as carbon dioxide and lactic acid.

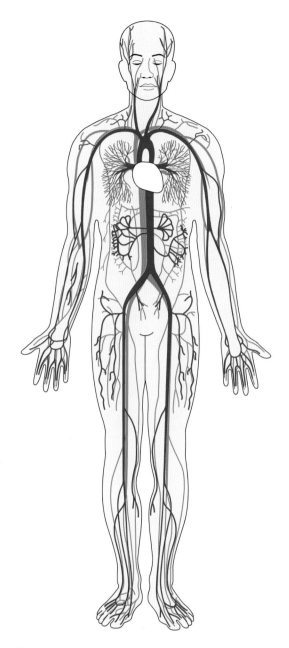

Figure 9.1 The cardiovascular system

Although this chapter looks at the cardiovascular system, there are clear links with the respiratory system, as this is how we receive the air containing oxygen into our bodies. The two systems together are known as the cardio-respiratory system.

The Heart

The heart works continuously throughout our lives. In an average life time it can beat over three billion times (try working it out: average heart rate (72 bpm) × number of minutes in a day × number of days in a year × average life expectancy (80). This is a resting value for the heart rate; if we exercise, it beats even more.

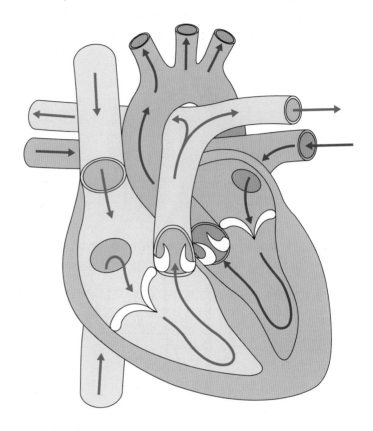

Figure 9.2 The heart

ACTION

There are ten components of the heart that you need to know:

- atria, ventricles, septum, tricuspid valve, bicuspid valve, semi-lunar valves, aorta, vena cava, pulmonary artery, pulmonary vein.

Using the description opposite, label the diagram in Figure 9.2.

The heart is made up of four chambers. The top two chambers are called **atria** and the bottom chambers are the **ventricles**. They are assigned a side, left or right. This is the first tricky bit. When labelling the heart you have to imagine that it is in your body when deciding which is left and right. Which is the right side of your body? If you were to look at a photograph of the side you have just identified, your right would appear to be your left! If you pick up the photograph and turn it to face the same way that you are facing, your right side is back where it belongs, on the right of your body. The same is true with the heart, so when you look at a diagram, do not forget to imagine it inside your body.

The left and right **atria** receive blood into the heart and pass it on to the **ventricles** when they contract.

The left atrium receives oxygenated blood from the lungs through the **pulmonary vein**, and the right atrium receives deoxygenated blood from the body through the **vena cava** (this is also a vein). Notice that atria is the plural form of atrium, ie you use it when talking about both atria rather than just one atrium.

Oxygenated means that the blood has picked up oxygen from the lungs (more on that in the next chapter). **Deoxygenated** means that the oxygen that was being carried by the blood has been removed or taken by the body's tissues to use to release energy.

The left and right **ventricles** receive blood from the atria above them; once they have received the blood they contract to force the blood out of the heart.

- The left ventricle has a thicker muscular wall because it has to do the most work; it is from here that blood is pumped out of the heart via the **aorta** to the rest of the body. The aorta is an artery.
- The right ventricle only pumps blood as far as the lungs, via the **pulmonary artery** to pick up more oxygen.

Three of the remaining four words that you need to know are all **valves**. Valves are flaps which only allow blood to flow one way, like emergency exit doors that hinge one way to let you out, but close after you so that you cannot go back the way you came.

If blood were allowed to flow backwards, it might not be pushed to the lungs to collect extra oxygen or be pumped around the body to the tissues that need to receive oxygenated blood. In other words, we would be unlikely to receive the oxygen we needed to complete exercise.

The **tricuspid valve** is on the right side of the heart (one way to remember this is to think of a saying like 'its all *right* to watch *TV*': TV stands for tricuspid valve, and it is on the right). It separates the right atrium from the right ventricle, allowing blood to flow from the atrium to the ventricle.

The **bicuspid valve** is on the left side of the heart separating the left atrium from the left ventricle. It allows blood to flow from the left atrium to the left ventricle but not the other way.

The remaining valves between the left ventricle and the aorta, and the right ventricle and the pulmonary artery, are called the **semi-lunar valves**. These valves allow the movement of blood from the ventricles out of the heart, but once it has left, the blood is not allowed to return.

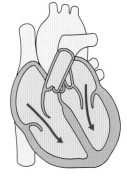

Figure 9.3 Ventricles fill with blood due to the contraction of the atria

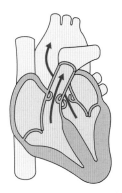

Figure 9.4 Ventricles contract to force blood out

QUESTION

If blood is oxygenated once it leaves the lungs, what has happened in the lungs?
If blood returning to the heart from the body is deoxygenated, what has happened to the oxygen?

QUESTION ?

Can you think why it is important that blood is not allowed to go back the way it has just come? What would happen when the ventricles contract if there were no valves between the ventricles and the atria?

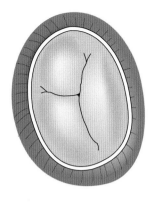

Figure 9.5 The valve controls the direction of the blood flow, when closed, no blood can flow through

The final label is the **septum**. This is the wall between the two sides of the heart, dividing left and right. This wall is required because the right side of the heart contains blood from the body which has been deoxygenated, whereas the blood on the left side of the heart contains oxygenated blood. If the blood were allowed to mix, the performer would receive a drop in the amount of oxygen being delivered to the muscles, so they would be unable to release as much energy for physical work.

You should now be able to finish labelling your diagram. Compare your answers with those shown in Figure 9.6

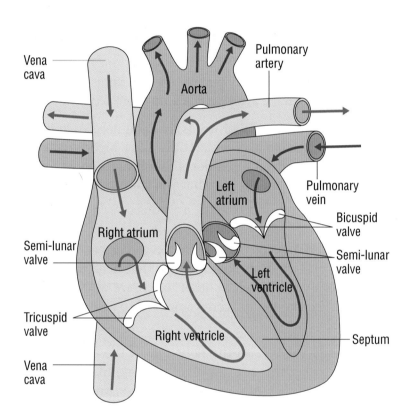

Figure 9.6 The heart

Double circulatory system

As the heart pumps, it circulates blood. Blood is circulated from the heart to the lungs and then back to the heart (circuit 1, the **pulmonary** circulation). Blood is also circulated from the heart to the rest of the body and back again (circuit 2, the **systemic** circulation). Because of these two clear areas that are circulated (lungs and the rest of the body), it is known as a double circulatory system.

ACTION

Starting with blood entering the heart from the body, take it in turns in your class to state the next stage of the circulation. You should say whether blood is entering or leaving and which vessel or chamber it enters or leaves through, as well as the valves involved, until you have completed the route of the blood in the double circulation.

Heart rate

Heart rate refers to the number of times the heart beats per minute. Each time the heart beats the ventricles contract, squeezing blood out of the heart into the lungs or the rest of the body. During exercise we need to increase the rate of blood flow, in other words, we need to make the blood flow faster so that we can deliver oxygen more quickly to the working muscles and remove waste products such as carbon dioxide at a quicker rate, so that the performer can keep working at a higher level of intensity than when they are at rest. This increase in blood flow is mainly achieved through increasing the heart rate.

ACTION

Working in pairs, measure each other's resting heart rate and make a note of it. Find your pulse and then count the number of times you feel the blood pulsate under your fingers in a minute.) You need to stay calm and quiet while your pulse is being measured as any movement or sudden noise will make your heart beat faster.

Take it in turns to carry out some exercise. This could be jumping up and down, or running on the spot for two minutes. Immediately after your exercise, ask your partner to measure your heart rate again and make a note of it. Then swap roles.

There should be a difference in your heart rate after exercise. Was it higher or lower? Why has your heart rate changed in this way?

Stroke volume

This is the amount of blood ejected from the heart per beat. When the ventricles contract, they do not empty completely of blood; only about 60 per cent of the blood is ejected. With exercise, the muscles of the wall of the heart surrounding the ventricles become stronger so that when they contract they can do so more forcibly. When this happens, they can squeeze harder on the blood in the ventricles and therefore push more out of the heart. This is why stroke volume increases with regular exercise. Think of a balloon filled with water: if you squeeze it a little bit a small amount of water comes out, but if you squeeze it harder, more water will be ejected.

The increase in stroke volume that is achieved through training also explains why fit performers tend to have lower resting heart rates than those who do not train.

? QUESTION

Looking at the equation below for cardiac output – can you work out why fit performers have lower resting heart rates than those who do not train?

Cardiac output

This is the amount of blood ejected from the heart per minute. It is calculated by multiplying heart rate (the number of times the heart beats per minute) by stroke volume (the amount of blood that is ejected from the heart per beat).

cardiac output = stroke volume × heart rate

At rest we need in the region of 5 litres of blood to circulate our bodies, but this figure can rise dramatically during exercise to 30 litres of blood per minute.

ACTION

What would the cardiac output be for a performer at rest with a heart rate of 70bpm and stroke volume of 70ml?

Blood vessels

Blood vessels carry blood to all the living cells in the body. There are different types of blood vessels: you need to know about **arteries**, **capillaries** and **veins**. Each type of blood vessel has a specific job to do, and is structured differently so that it can do its job effectively.

Arteries

These carry blood away from the heart, which is easy to remember as **a**way and **a**rteries both start with the letter **A**. Also helping us is the fact that the **a**orta, the main artery, also starts with an **A**.

Arteries are made up of three layers: the outside layer is tough, the middle layer is muscular and the inner layer is smooth to make it easy for the blood to pass through.

? QUESTION

Look at the two images of Kelly Holmes: in Figure 9.7 she is resting after completing her race, and in Figure 9.8 she is in the middle of her event.

While she is running she will need to deliver more oxygen to her muscles than when she is at rest. She will also need to remove the increased carbon dioxide that is being created during exercise, therefore she needs to increase her cardiac output. Remember, cardiac output = stroke volume × heart rate. What, therefore, are the two ways she can increase her cardiac output?

Figure 9.7 Kelly Holmes celebrating after her event

Figure 9.8 Kelly Holmes in action

Things to remember about arteries:

- They carry blood away from the heart.
- They carry blood at higher pressure than the other vessels because they take blood from the heart.
- They have thick muscular walls.
- They pulsate: when the heart relaxes, the artery muscle contracts, pushing the blood forward.
- Because they carry blood away from the heart they carry oxygenated blood (there is ONE exception to this, see the question below).

QUESTION ?

What is the name of the artery which carries deoxygenated blood away from the heart?

Veins

Veins carry blood back to the heart. The main vein is called the **vena cava**.

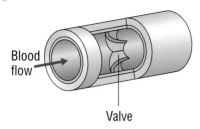

Blood flow

Valve

Figure 9.9 A vein

Things to remember about veins:

- They carry blood towards the heart.
- They carry blood at low pressure.
- They have valves.
- They have thin walls.
- They have a larger internal lumen (the space in the middle of the vessel) than arteries.
- Because they carry blood back to the heart, they carry deoxygenated blood (there is ONE exception to this; see the question below)

Capillaries

If arteries take blood away from the heart and veins bring it back, how does the blood get from the artery into the vein? Via **capillaries**, the vessels which form the link between the other two. This is where carbon dioxide will diffuse from the tissues into the blood, and oxygen will diffuse from the blood to the tissues. See Figure 9.10: the fine network of blood vessels between the larger two are the capillaries.

 **QUESTION**

What is the name of the vein which carries oxygenated blood to the heart?

Things to remember about capillaries:

- They are the link between arteries and veins.
- They are one cell thick and very fragile.
- Blood cells pass through them one cell at a time (giving time for the exchange of gases to take place).

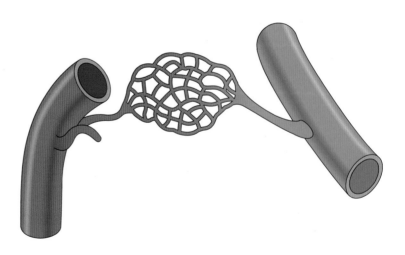

Figure 9.10 Capillaries between the larger blood vessels

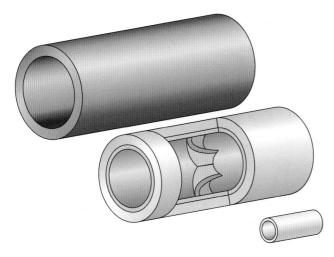

Figure 9.11 Arteries, capillaries and veins

 **QUESTION**

Can you work out which of the blood vessels in Figure 9.11 is which, from the information given about arteries, capillaries and veins?

ACTION

Use the descriptions of the blood vessels in this chapter to help you decide whether the following descriptions are of arteries, capillaries or veins:

1. I always travel away from the heart.
2. I am the link between the other two types of blood vessels.
3. I have thin walls.
4. I normally carry oxygenated blood.
5. I have thick muscular walls.
6. I have a small lumen (the lumen is the space in the middle of the vessel).
7. I allow the exchange of gases and nutrients with the cells of the body.
8. I always travel towards the heart.
9. I pulsate.
10. I work under high pressure.

The blood

Blood is made up of red blood cells, white blood cells, platelets and plasma. Adults have around 5.5 litres of blood circulating their bodies. **Plasma** is the liquid part of the blood; it is mainly made up of water. If the plasma did not exist, the solid cells would not be able to flow around the body, so the plasma gives the other cells a ride.

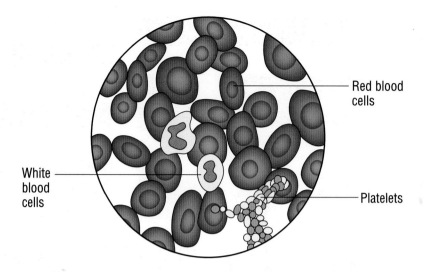

Figure 9.12 Blood cells

Red blood cells

These are very important to a performer. The red blood cells contain haemoglobin, a substance which allows the transportation of oxygen around the body. In blood doping and the use of EPO, mentioned in Chapter 6, the performer increases the number of red blood cells they have in their blood so that they can carry more oxygen to aid their performance, despite the risk of unhealthy side effects.

White blood cells

These are also very important to the performer. They are responsible for seeking out and destroying infections. The white cells can slide through the walls of the blood vessel and attack bacteria at the site of the infection. The white blood cells keep the athlete healthy.

Platelets

These play a vital role in maintaining the health of a sports performer. Platelets aid clotting: if the performer receives a cut or a graze, platelets are dispatched to put a plug in the hole in the skin so that there is no further blood loss.

ACTION

Complete the crossword on the cardiovascular system.

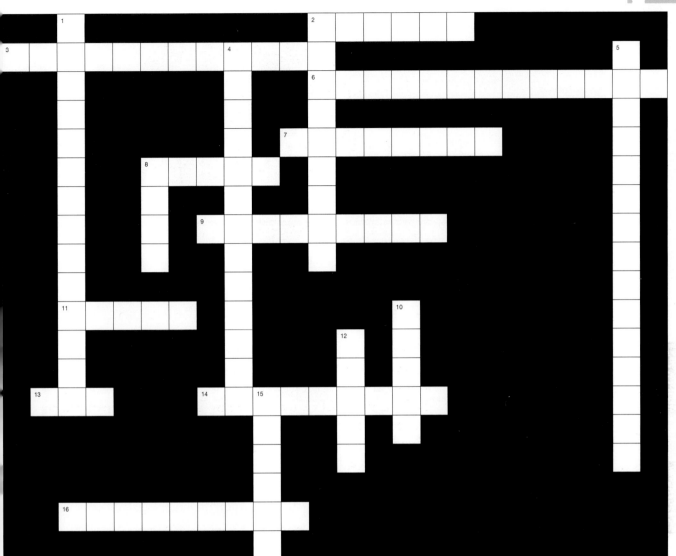

Across:

2 What type of circulatory systems do humans have?

3 What is being defined? 'The amount of blood leaving the heart per beat'

6 If I increase stroke volume, what else will increase? (7, 6)

7 Main vein in the body, brings blood back to the heart (4, 4)

8 What is the name of the structure that stops blood flowing the wrong way?

9 What happens to the heart rate during exercise?

11 The chambers in the top half of the heart

13 Which blood cells carry oxygen to help the performer work for longer?

14 Which term is represented in this equation as a question mark? Cardiac output = ? × SV (5, 4)

16 Which blood vessel has this characteristic? Only allows blood to pass through one cell at a time

Down:

1 Found on the right side of the heart, it prevents the back flow of blood (9, 5)

2 What happens to the resting heart rate as a result of regular training

4 The strongest of the muscular walls around the chambers of the heart

5 Takes deoxygenated blood away from the heart

8 Which blood vessel has very thin walls?

10 Which blood cells protect the performer from infection?

12 Takes oxygenated blood away from the heart

15 Which blood vessel has a thick muscular wall?

GOALS

By the end of this section you should be able to:

- ☐ identify the positions of the components of the respiratory system
- ☐ describe the function of the nasal passages and lungs
- ☐ describe the mechanics of inspiration and expiration
- ☐ describe the biomechanical aspects of respiration
- ☐ state and explain the relative composition of inhaled and exhaled air
- ☐ explain the terms oxygen debt, vital capacity and tidal volume and the effect of exercise on them
- ☐ explain the difference between aerobic and anaerobic activities
- ☐ explain why lactic acid is produced.

In the previous chapter we looked at the importance of the circulatory system in transporting blood carrying oxygen to our working muscles (and the rest of the body). The respiratory system is also vital to the performer, because without it the performer would not be able to receive air (containing oxygen) into the body for the circulatory system to circulate, nor would it be able to expel carbon dioxide from the body. These are the main functions of the lungs.

Composition of inspired and expired air

Figure 10.1 shows the relative percentages of gases in the air we breathe in.

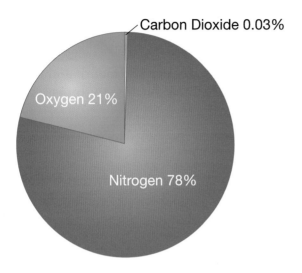

Carbon Dioxide 0.03%

Oxygen 21%

Nitrogen 78%

Figure 10.1 Percentages of gases in inspired air

As you can see from Figure 10.1, the air we breathe in is approximately 78 per cent nitrogen, 21 per cent oxygen, and 0.03 per cent carbon dioxide. Traces of water vapour are also present but the figure will vary depending on the weather. (Not surprisingly, if it is raining there is more water vapour in the air.) For your course you need to know if any of these values change and, if they do, the reason why they change.

There are some traces of other gases in air as well, but these are in very small amounts (and not on your course). It is useful to know they exist though as this explains why, when you add up the percentages of oxygen, carbon dioxide and nitrogen in air they do not equal 100 per cent. The missing points of a percentage are due to the traces of these other gases.

We all need oxygen to release energy, but when participating in physical activity we need more, because we need more energy. The efficiency of the respiratory system in getting oxygen into the body, and the circulatory system in delivering it where it is needed, will have a big impact on the level of performance achieved in most sporting activities. For example, imagine the 1500 metre runner who could only walk or do a slow jog because they could not breathe enough oxygen into their bodies to provide enough energy to go any faster, or the basketball player who could sprint down the court once on a fast break, but then had to sit out of the match for ten minutes while he recovered – neither performer would be competitively successful in their sports.

Components of the respiratory system

To begin with we need to consider the components of the respiratory system and the route the air takes to reach the lungs for gas exchange to take place. Figure 10.2 is a diagram of the human respiratory system and shows the labels you need to learn.

Air enters the body by passing through the **mouth** and **nasal passages (nose)**. It is much better to breathe in through the nose than the mouth because:

- the nose has a filter system to remove dust particles from the air
- it also warms the air so that it matches body temperature
- it moistens the air so that it arrives in the lungs saturated with water to aid the respiration process.

On leaving the nasal passages, the air flows into the **larynx** – this is the bump you can feel on your neck, where you can easily feel your pulse if you place two fingers together and gently press just to the side of it. (If you can feel a pulse, are your fingers on an artery, vein or capillary?)

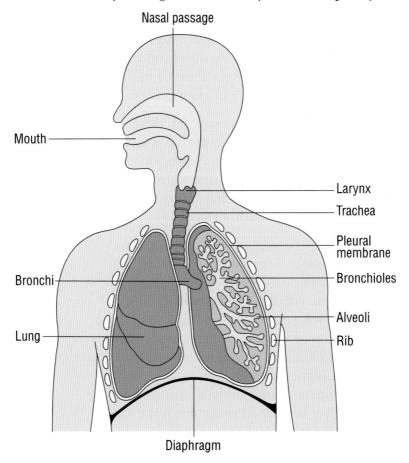

Figure 10.2 The Respiratory System

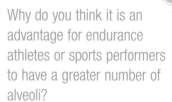

QUESTION ?

Why do you think it is an advantage for endurance athletes or sports performers to have a greater number of alveoli?

Figure 10.3 Endurance athletes have very efficient respiratory systems so that oxygen can be used to release energy for longer

After the larynx, the air goes through the trachea, into the right or left **bronchus** (if you are talking about both, the plural word is **bronchi**). From the bronchi the air travels on to the **bronchioles** and finally on to the **alveoli**.

The alveoli are very important; it is here that the exchange of gases takes place. Gaseous exchange is the swapping of oxygen and carbon dioxide due to the pressure gradients of each of the gases at the site of the exchange. For example, the percentage of oxygen in the lungs is much higher than that in the blood vessels arriving at the lungs. Due to the

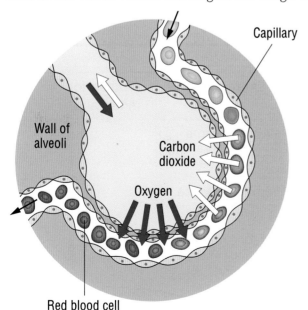

Figure 10.4 Oxygen can be seen leaving the alveolus (singular of alveoli) and carbon dioxide entering from the blood

pressure difference (gradient), the oxygen diffuses from the lungs to the blood. Meanwhile, the percentage of carbon dioxide in the blood is higher than that in the lungs, and so this gas diffuses from the blood to the lungs. The gases are therefore 'swapped'.

Regular endurance training will result in an increase in the number of alveoli present in the lungs, and an increase in the number of capillaries that are available to exchange gases with them.

An increase in alveoli means that the performer can diffuse more oxygen into the blood, provided that the alveoli have access to a blood supply for the exchange of gases (see Figure 10.4). This is why there is an increase in the number of capillaries available. These two factors combined will lead to greater oxygen uptake during exercise, and therefore potentially more oxygen available to release energy, helping to fuel exercise for longer.

? QUESTION

From the work you have already completed, you will know that we use oxygen to release energy. What do you think happens to the level of oxygen breathed out, compared with the percentage breathed in? Carbon dioxide needs to be removed from the body because it is produced during exercise as part of the process that releases energy; therefore, what do you think happens to the carbon dioxide levels? Nitrogen is neither used nor created by the body, so what will happen to its levels? Finally, water vapour is released during the process of energy release, therefore what would you expect to happen to the level of water vapour in air that is breathed out? Look at Table 10.1 for a comparison of the values of the gases and water vapour in air that are inspired (breathed in) and expired (breathed out). Does it match your answers?

Component	Inspired air (%)	Expired air (%)	Difference	Reason for difference
Nitrogen	78	78	Stays the same	
Oxygen	21	17	Drop in value	
Carbon dioxide	0.03	4	Increase in value	
Water vapour	Varies	Saturated	Increase in value	

Table 10.1 Composition of inspired and expired air

Expiration and inspiration

We have seen the path that the air must take en route to the lungs, but what do we physically do to help us breathe in and out? The movement of the **diaphragm** and the **ribs** helps the movement of air into and out of the lungs.

During **expiration** (breathing out), the lungs slightly deflate (like a balloon losing some of the air inside it); when this happens the lungs do not take up as much room and so the ribs can move downwards and inwards and the diaphragm can relax (move up). This helps the lungs to expel some of the air inside them.

During **inspiration** (breathing in) however, the lungs need to expand so they can hold more air, like a balloon being inflated. In order to make room for the lungs to do this, the diaphragm contracts (this pulls it tight and flat, see Figure 10.5), and the ribs move up and out due to the contraction of the external intercostal muscles (these attach one rib to the rib below it – the muscle runs downwards from the upper rib and fowards to the rib below).

During exercise, the ventilation rate increases: an average adult male will inspire and expire between 10 to 14 times a minute at rest, but this can increase to 25 times a minute during heavy exercise. Try measuring your breathing rate by placing your hands across your chest (opposite hand to opposite shoulder) and counting the rise and fall of the rib cage. It is difficult to count accurately, but you should be able to feel a difference while at rest and immediately after exercise.

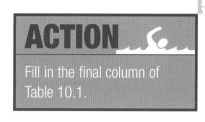
ACTION

Fill in the final column of Table 10.1.

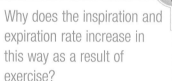

QUESTION ?

Why does the inspiration and expiration rate increase in this way as a result of exercise?

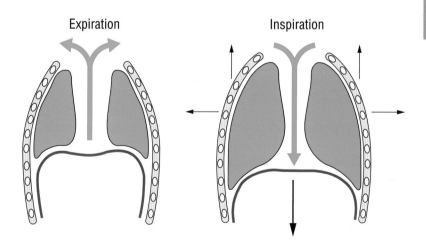

Expiration   Inspiration

Figure 10.5 Movement of ribs and diaphragm during expiration and inspiration

Lung volumes

The average adult human can hold about six litres of air in their lungs.

- **Tidal volume** is the movement of air into and out of the lungs in one normal breath (about half a litre of air).

- **Vital capacity** is the maximum amount of air that can be expired after a maximal inspiration.

Although the lungs do not respond to regular training, ie they do not increase in size, intensive exercise will fatigue the diaphragm and the external intercostal muscles so that they become stronger and more able to cope with the work a sports performer is doing. Due to the increased strength of these muscles, **tidal volume** can be increased.

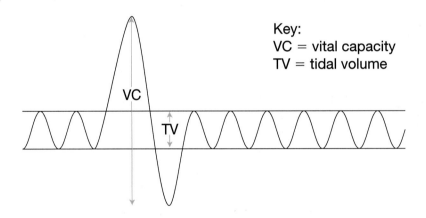

Key:
VC = vital capacity
TV = tidal volume

Figure 10.6 Vital capacity and tidal volume of a performer at rest

? QUESTION

What would you expect to happen to the lines for tidal volume in Figure 10.6 once the performer started to exercise?

Aerobic and anaerobic respiration

Aerobic respiration

In this chapter and the last, it has been stated that the body needs oxygen, and more is needed when we exercise. What is the reason for this?

In order for us to do any physical work, we need energy. This energy is released from the food we eat. Energy can be released using oxygen (**aerobic**) or without using oxygen (**anaerobic**). More energy is released if oxygen is present, therefore in aerobic activities (remember those? See Chapter 5) the more oxygen supplied to the tissues, the better.

Glucose (from carbohydrates) is broken down in our tissues in the presence of oxygen to release energy. This is represented by the equation shown in Figure 10.7.

$$C_6H_{12}O_6 + 6O_2 \quad \text{Gives} \quad 6CO_2 + 6H_2O + \text{ENERGY}$$

$$\underset{\text{GLUCOSE}}{} \quad \underset{\text{OXYGEN}}{} \qquad \underset{\substack{\text{CARBON} \\ \text{DIOXIDE}}}{} \quad \underset{\text{WATER}}{}$$

Figure 10.7 Energy equation

ACTION

This equation should help explain a lot! Have a look at the equation; write down any facts which you can work out from it before looking at the list below.

During aerobic respiration.

- energy is released from respiration
- glucose is needed
- oxygen is needed
- carbon dioxide is produced
- water is produced.

By looking at this equation we can see why

- oxygen levels go down
- carbon dioxide levels go up
- levels of water vapour increase.

We saw from the equation that oxygen is used to release energy. However, if the level of exercise is too intense, oxygen cannot be supplied quickly enough to release energy in this way. When this happens, we release energy anaerobically (see Chapter 5).

Anaerobic respiration

This may last for a short period of time, but when we rely on this method of energy release, **lactic acid** is also produced. Due to the increased acidity in the muscle cell and blood, the muscles become fatigued; the performer will need time to recover before continuing at the same intensity of physical work. For example, a sprinter doing interval training will complete their sprint and stop, allowing themselves time to recover before completing another set. Games players who have just sprinted for the ball to reach it before their opponent will recover by jogging back into position, once they have passed the ball on. During this recovery period the performer will still be breathing heavily even though they are not working hard. This is so that they can repay the **oxygen debt** they have developed. An oxygen debt is the amount of oxygen consumed during recovery, above that which would normally have been used at rest; it results from a shortfall in availability of oxygen during exercise.

This additional oxygen is used to restock oxygen levels in the muscles and tissues, and to help break down any lactic acid that has formed.

? QUESTION

When the athlete finishes his run, will his breathing rate go back to his resting rate straight away? Explain your answer. What is the term used to describe this effect?

ACTION

Rearrange the words in Table 10.2 to give the correct route through the respiratory system.

Bronchioles	Nasal passage	Ribs up and out	Expiration
Exchange of gases	Diaphragm up	Larynx	Inspiration
Ribs down and in	Bronchi	Lungs	Trachea
	Alveoli	Diaphragm down	

Table 10.2 Aspects of the respiratory system

1 _____   2 _____

3 _____   4 _____

5 _____   6 _____

7 _____   8 _____

9 _____   10 _____

11 _____   12 _____

12 _____   14 _____

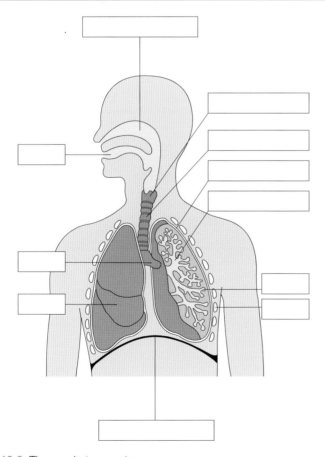

Figure 10.8 The respiratory system

Figure 10.9 Changing levels of oxygen and carbon dioxide during exercise

ACTION

Shade in the containers of oxygen and carbon dioxide in Figure 10.9 to show what happens to the quantities of these gases as blood circulates around the athlete's body during exercise. The containers are numbered; number 1 is at the lungs, number 2 part way around the circulation and so on until the blood has completed its circuit back to the lungs at number 6.

chapter eleven
THE SKELETAL SYSTEM (BONES)

GOALS

By the end of this section you should be able to:

☐ describe the process of ossification and identify the composition of bones

☐ discuss the growth and development of bone

☐ state the functions of the skeleton and discuss the importance of bones and the skeleton to sporting performance

☐ identify the main bones of the skeleton

☐ classify the bones of the skeleton and relate their function to sporting performance.

The skeleton gives us our shape and, with the help of joints and muscles, allows us to move. It is for this reason that we need to study this topic for GCSE PE. We have over 200 bones in our bodies; fortunately you only have to know the names of and identify 21 of them.

Bone development

Occasionally in physical activity, despite taking reasonable safety precautions, some sports performers break bones. However, considering the number of people who take part in sport this does not happen frequently, as bone is made from strong material.

When you were born your bones would still have been developing from cartilage through a process called **ossification**. Bones develop over time from pre-birth into adult life. This is fortunate as it means that if broken or fractured, bones can be repaired. We can even increase their

Figure 11.1 The length of your bones will determine how tall you grow

strength by following an appropriate exercise programme (one that involves weight-bearing activities such as jogging or walking) and eating a balanced diet (see Chapter 6). We need to be able to make our bones grow stronger so that they can physically support our larger size as we grow older. Bones do stop growing in length however (but only eventually in the case of the basketball player in Figure 11.1); this is why you do not grow taller throughout your adult life. If not, imagine how tall the basketball player in the figure would be by the age of 40!

Formation of long bones

Ossification begins a few weeks after conception and continues into early adult life. The periostium (like a skin around the bone), the spongy bone found in the centre of the diaphysis (bone shaft) and the compact bone at the edges of the diaphysis form during this first phase of ossification, normally before birth. After birth, the second phase of ossification occurs in the epiphyses (the ends of the long bone). The cartilage is gradually replaced with spongy bone until it has all been replaced except for two areas:

- where the bone forms a joint with another bone (see Chapter 12)
- at the **epiphyseal** line (growth region).

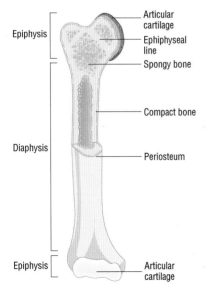

Figure 11.2 Long bone

Four functions of the skeleton

The skeleton:

1. Gives the body its shape and supports us in an upright position. This is vital for sporting performance.

2. Protects the body's vital organs.

   The role of the skeleton to protect vital organs is very important in sport. For example: the ribs and sternum protect the heart and lungs if a batsman is struck with a cricket ball, the cranium protects the brain from head injury in rugby during tackles or racket injury in squash (if the opposition has a wide swing); the pelvic girdle protects the intestines if there is a misplaced punch in boxing.

3. Allows movement through the use of joints and muscle attachment. Most sports involve a lot of movement; eg squash, football and netball would be impossible to play if we were unable to use any of our muscles to move our bones.

4. Blood production (red blood cells, white blood cells and platelets). This function is also relevant to the sports performer as we saw in the previous chapter. Red blood cells carry oxygen; the performer needs a good supply of oxygen to release energy. White blood cells are important to keep the performer healthy so that they can perform at their best. Platelets are also important to help the clotting of cuts, so that players are allowed to continue to play rather than be substituted.

ACTION

Look at the images in figure 11.3. Which organs would be protected by the bones of the skeleton indicated by the arrows?

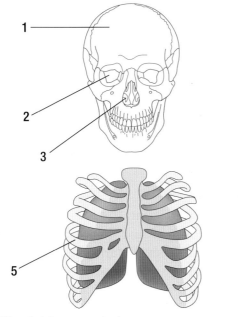

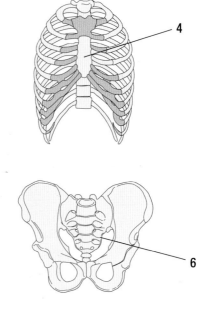

Figure 11.3 The skeleton as protector

The bones of the skeleton

Figure 11.4 shows diagrams of the human skeleton.

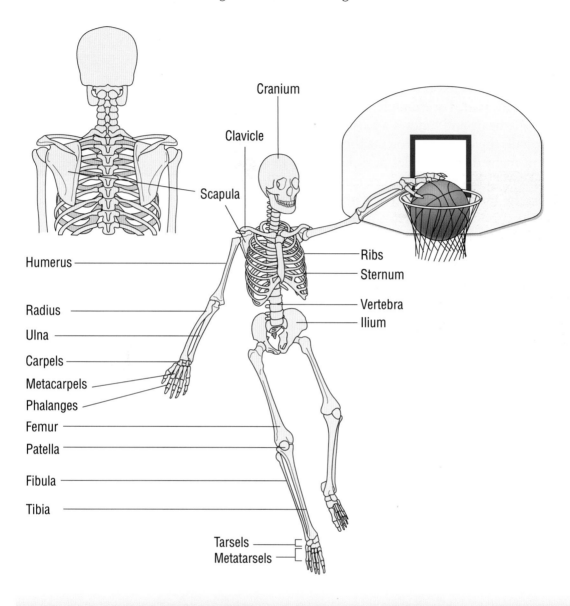

Cranium

Clavicle

Scapula

Humerus

Radius

Ulna

Carpels

Metacarpels

Phalanges

Femur

Patella

Fibula

Tibia

Ribs

Sternum

Vertebra

Ilium

Tarsels

Metatarsels

Figure 11.4 The human skeleton

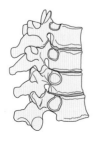

Figure 11.5 Vertebral discs

The vertebral column

This is made up of five regions; the bones in each of the regions are of different sizes and shapes, and are all irregular bones. For example, the bones start off relatively small at the neck, and increase in size as they need to support more of the body weight. Although the **atlas** and **axis** of the **cervical** region allow specific movements, the remaining vertebrae of

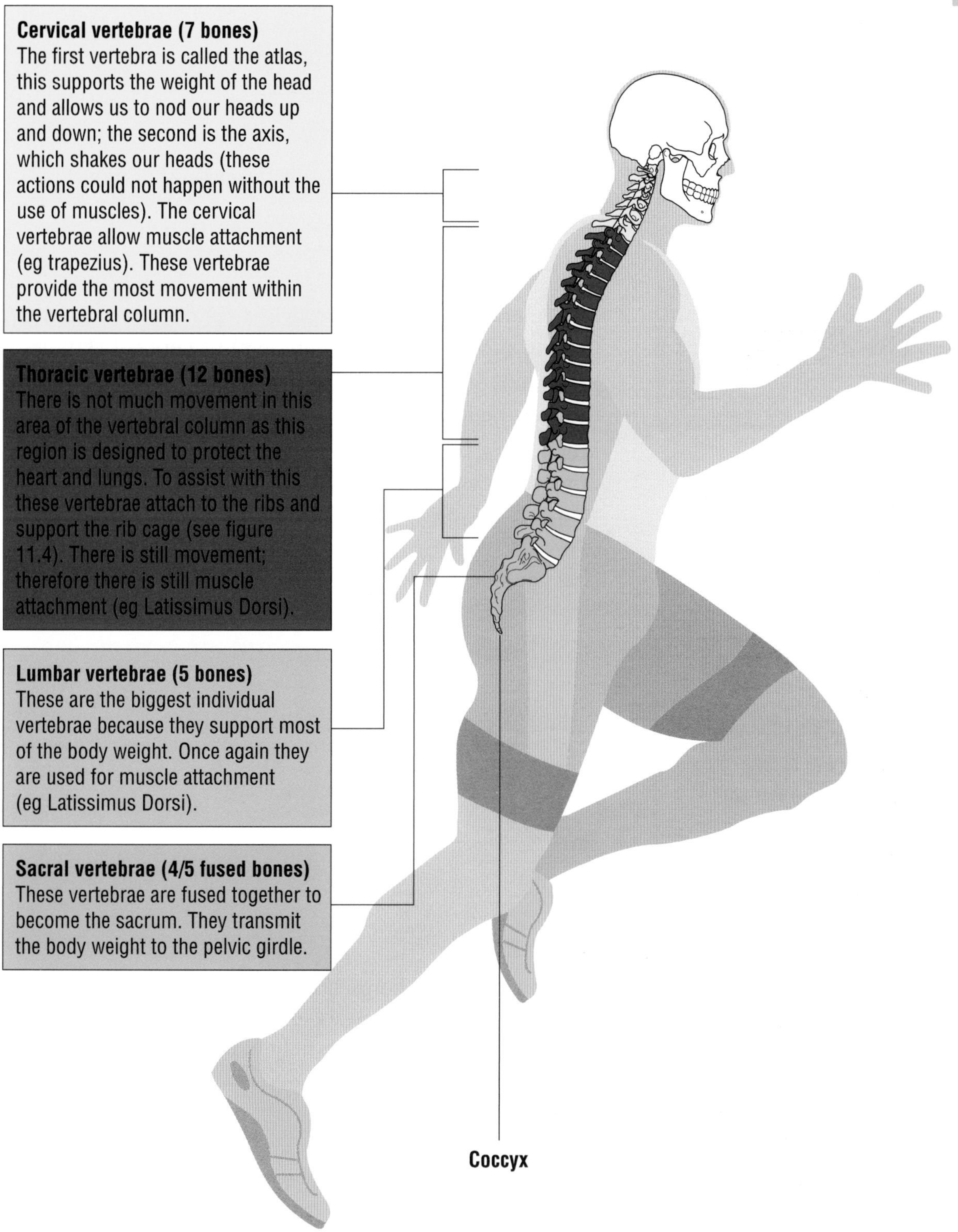

Cervical vertebrae (7 bones)
The first vertebra is called the atlas, this supports the weight of the head and allows us to nod our heads up and down; the second is the axis, which shakes our heads (these actions could not happen without the use of muscles). The cervical vertebrae allow muscle attachment (eg trapezius). These vertebrae provide the most movement within the vertebral column.

Thoracic vertebrae (12 bones)
There is not much movement in this area of the vertebral column as this region is designed to protect the heart and lungs. To assist with this these vertebrae attach to the ribs and support the rib cage (see figure 11.4). There is still movement; therefore there is still muscle attachment (eg Latissimus Dorsi).

Lumbar vertebrae (5 bones)
These are the biggest individual vertebrae because they support most of the body weight. Once again they are used for muscle attachment (eg Latissimus Dorsi).

Sacral vertebrae (4/5 fused bones)
These vertebrae are fused together to become the sacrum. They transmit the body weight to the pelvic girdle.

Coccyx

Figure 11.6 The vertebral column

the cervical, **thoracic** and **lumbar** regions all contribute to the movements possible at the spine, as they are jointed (see Figure 11.6). These movements are:

ACTION

Look at the images in Figure 11.7. Discuss with a partner how the vertebral column assists these performers in their activities. Think about the role of the different parts of the vertebral column and the functions they have as part of the spine, and the skeleton.

- flexion (bending forward)
- extension (bending backwards)
- lateral flexion (bending sideways)
- rotation (twisting and turning).

Discs of cartilage 'sit' between the vertebrae that move (Figure 11.5).

Use of the vertebral column in sport

- Movement of the head to aid technique (spotting landing, looking at track, tucking up in dive) by cervical vertebrae.
- Protection of heart and lungs by thoracic vertebrae when three of the four performers 'land'.
- Muscle attachment to allow the performers to flex, extend or rotate as required by their technique.
- Weight bearing for the sprinter (and for other three performers leading up their aspect of flight, eg run up for pole vault) by the sacral vertebrae.

Classification and function of bones

All of the bones of the human skeleton can be classified according to their function. Bones are either:

- long
- short
- flat
- irregular.

Long bones

Bones are called long bones if they are longer in length than they are wide. These bones act as levers in the body, allowing us to move (with the help of muscles and joints).

Short bones

These are box-shaped, in that they tend to be as long as they are wide. Do any of the bones in Figure 11.4 fit this description? Fill in your table. These bones are specially designed for strength or weight bearing, and absorbing shock (eg running, handstands and other inverted balances or movements in gymnastics).

? QUESTION

Create a table with columns headed by the different types of bone: short, long, flat, irregular. Look at Figure 11.4. Which of the bones are long bones according to that description? Put your answers in your table.

ACTION

See if your PE or Science department have a skeleton or parts of a skeleton that you can look at. Try to tell the difference between the bones and classify them without looking at the list you have already completed.

Figure 11.7

Flat bones

These bones are normally flat, thin and curved; can you see any of these in Figure 11.4? Put your answers in your table. These bones give protection and a large surface area for muscle attachment.

Irregular bones

Irregular bones are also used for protection and muscle attachment.

Look back at Figure 11.4; are there any bones that you haven't been able to classify yet? Could these be irregular bones? If the shape of the bone doesn't fit any of the other descriptions then it probably is irregular. Put your answers in your table.

There are two common errors or difficulties in learning the names of the bones of the skeleton.

1. Sometimes it is difficult to remember which of the bones is which in the lower leg. If you are having difficulty with this it might be helpful to remember that the **t**ibia is the **t**hicker of the two bones, and that the **f**ibula is the **f**iner (or 'f'inner!) of the two bones. It is also worth pointing out that you must make sure you do not confuse the endings of the names of these bones.

2. A similar problem occurs with remembering the bones of the lower arm. In this case, try to remember that the **r**adius is the **r**ight bone for the thumb; provided the diagram you are asked to label has the hand on it as well, this should not be a problem!

ACTION

Once you have become familiar with the names of these bones, copy each of their names onto sticky labels and place them on a friend to help reinforce your understanding of the correct location of each bone.

ACTION

To assist you in becoming familiar with the names of the bones you need to know, find and circle them in the grid below.

I	Q	T	M	V	F	S	H	C	I	A	X	P	A	E
L	L	H	X	E	L	T	E	N	V	L	P	H	B	C
I	D	L	M	A	T	R	C	T	I	U	A	A	P	W
U	Y	U	S	J	V	A	Y	T	S	P	T	L	V	H
M	R	R	T	I	P	H	T	R	W	A	E	A	W	D
E	A	Q	C	I	Q	R	U	A	O	C	L	N	Y	D
T	L	A	L	U	B	I	F	M	R	S	L	G	G	Q
X	L	C	R	A	N	I	U	M	E	S	A	E	N	G
R	Y	Q	I	P	N	L	A	S	R	R	A	S	Y	M
A	R	C	U	V	A	L	T	T	R	R	U	L	O	Q
B	V	W	C	R	A	E	U	B	Z	L	G	S	S	O
M	V	Y	C	O	R	L	C	I	C	A	R	O	H	T
U	S	A	H	N	C	K	C	R	A	D	I	U	S	G
L	S	Y	U	L	W	L	B	O	J	P	X	D	G	F
M	L	M	Q	M	K	M	E	D	A	M	S	B	I	R

CERVICAL	ILIUM	SACRAL
CLAVICLE	LUMBAR	SCAPULA
COCCYX	METATARSALS	STERNUM
CRANIUM	PATELLA	TARSALS
FEMUR	PHALANGES	THORACIC
FIBULA	RADIUS	TIBIA
HUMERUS	RIBS	ULNA

chapter twelve
JOINTS, TENDONS AND LIGAMENTS

GOALS

By the end of this chapter you should be able to:

☐ define the term 'joint' and explain its use in sport

☐ identify the bones of the elbow, knee, hip and shoulder joints

☐ state the components of a joint and the role of each component (including ligaments and tendons)

☐ classify joints as hinge, pivot or ball and socket and link to possible joint actions.

ACTION

Using your knowledge from the previous chapter, and specifically Figure 11.4, identify the occasions where two or more bones meet.

ACTION

Use the images of the skeleton in the previous chapter to help you fill in the empty column on Table 12.1. List the bones that make the joint.

What is a joint?

Joints are responsible for 'fitting' the skeleton together, along with ligaments. A need for strength makes the bones rigid, but if the skeleton consisted of one solid bone, movement would be impossible. The definition that you need to learn of a joint is:

A place where two or more bones meet.

The areas you should have identified in the Action above will all be joints. For this course you only need to know the joints listed in Table 12.1. For the purpose of this activity I

Name of joint	Bones that make up the joint
Elbow	
Shoulder	
Hip	
Knee	
Neck	

Table 12.1 Bones and joints

have called this joint the neck. Although the joint is found within the neck, you would not normally use this term to describe the location of this joint (see Table 12.2).

Check your answers with those in Table 12.2. It is possible that you might have added a couple of extra bones to some of the joints. Only the bones that actually articulate (meet) with each other form the joint.

Name of joint	Bones that make up the joint	Image of the joint
Elbow	Humerus, radius and ulna (Joint 1) and radius and ulna (Joint 2)	
Shoulder	Humerus Scapula	
Hip	Femur Hip (the fused bones of the ilium, ischium and pubis, but you do not need to know this for GCSE level)	

Table 12.2 Bones and joints

Name of joint	Bones that make up the joint	Image of the joint
Knee	Femur Tibia (Although the fibula is next to the tibia it is not involved in the movement at the joint. Similarly, the patella is there to protect the front of the joint)	
Neck	Atlas Axis (This is the name commonly given to this joint rather than neck)	

Table 12.2 Bones and joints *continued*

The shoulder joint is the most freely moveable in the body. This obviously presents an advantage in terms of sport – look at the arm action in the butterfly stroke for swimming, or the bowling action in cricket, both demand a high level of mobility. You cannot achieve this amount of movement with any other limb. The disadvantage is that it is a relatively unstable joint, ie can dislocate.

The knee joint is most likely to cause problems in later life due to overuse in sport. It is put under a great deal of pressure from pounding when running and turning, and from the knocks it receives in contact sports. Knee injuries are most common in sports that require twisting movements and sudden changes of direction, eg football, rugby, basketball, netball and skiing.

The components of a synovial joint

Figure 12.1 is a diagram of a typical synovial joint and its related structures (in this case the knee). All synovial joints have the same components and supporting structures. These are:

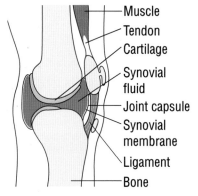

Figure 12.1 Components of a synovial joint

- **Muscle**: this is needed to move the bones (see Chapter 13).

- **Tendons**: these attach muscles to bones. They are very tough as they have to withstand the force of the muscle contraction required to move the bone; they are also flexible so that they can cope with the flexion and extension of the muscle (see movement at joints on page 140). If there is sudden exertion, tendons can snap or tear; if this is the Achilles tendon (at the heel) the performer will be out of action for weeks or longer. Tendons can also become inflamed, making further use of the muscle painful. The condition is called tendonitis and is normally associated with overuse, eg where a sports performer has increased their training intensity a bit too quickly.

- **Cartilage**: protects the ends of the bone from friction.

- **Joint capsule**: this is the tough outer layer that surrounds the joint. The capsule 'sticks' to the periostium of the bones that form the joint.

- **Synovial membrane**: this lines the joint capsule and seals it. The synovial membrane secretes synovial fluid.

- **Synovial fluid**: this is a clear fluid which lubricates the joint.

- **Ligaments**: these join bone to bone. They stabilise the joint by supporting it and limiting its movement, helping to prevent dislocation and movements that might result in breaks of the bone to which they are attached. They are slightly elastic and can stretch during a long exercise session, making the joint slightly less stable. However, once the performer has rested, the ligament will normally return to its original length. The ligaments in the ankle and knee often suffer sprains.

- **Bone**: the place where two or more bones meet is the site of the joint.

ACTION

Fill the gaps in the following statements about the components of joints using the words from Table 12.3. You can use the words more than once, or not at all.

Overuse	Synovial	Move	Cartilage	Achilles
Bones	Joint	Fluid	Tendons	Capsule
		Membrane	Ligaments	

Table 12.3 Components of joints

1. Muscles are needed to make the bone [   ].

2. [   ] join bone to bone.

3. [   ] attach muscle to bone.

4. The [   ] [   ] secretes [   ] [   ].

5. Tendonitis is an [   ] injury.

6. [   ] meet to form a joint.

7. The [   ] [   ] surrounds the joint.

8. [   ] protects the ends of the bones.

9. The [   ] stabilise the joint.

10. The [   ] tendon is found at the heel of the foot.

Classification of joints

You need to be able to classify the joints listed in Table 12.1 as either:

- hinge (elbow and knee)
- pivot (atlas and axis)
- ball and socket (hip and shoulder).

(There are other joint types, but these are not currently part of your course.)

Joints are classified into certain **types** depending on the amount of movement that can be carried out at them; eg the movement possible at your knee is different from the movement possible at the shoulder.

ACTION

Look at the five joints in Table 12.2. Try out some movements, taking each joint in turn: what can you do with each of them? Can any of the joints do similar movements? Is there one type of movement that they can all do? You should be able to 'pair' two sets of the joints together as they allow the same type of movement. Which of the joints in Table 12.4 go together, and which is the odd one out?

atlas, axis (neck)		shoulder
elbow	hip	knee

Table 12.4 Groups of joints

Movement at joints

The reason you need to know for your course that there are different types of joints is that the type of joint will determine the type of **movement** we can do at that joint.

Movements at joints are known as **joint actions** and are given specific names, as shown in Table 12.5.

Joint Action	Description of Action	Example from sport	Explanation
Flexion	Bending a limb at a joint		The elbow of the ball handler is bent

Table 12.5 Joint actions

Joint Action	Description of Action	Example from sport	Explanation
Extension	Straightening a limb at a joint		The arm holding the discus is straight
Abduction	Movement of a limb sideways away from the centre of the body		The gymnast's legs have been moved sideways away from the centre of the body
Adduction	Movement of a limb sideways towards the centre of the body		The gymnast's legs have moved together

Table 12.5 Joint actions *continued*

Joint Action	Description of Action	Example from sport	Explanation
Rotation	Circular movement around the joint		The swimmer's arms make a circular action to complete the butterfly stroke

Table 12.5 Joint action *continued*

ACTION

Think about the movement at the shoulder, knee, atlas and axis again. This time, give an example in Table 12.6 of a named joint action (flexion, extension and so on) that you can do at each of them, rather than just a description of the movement. Give a different joint action for each joint.

Joint	Joint action
Knee	
Shoulder	
Atlas, axis	

Table 12.6 Joint actions

You can see examples of the different joint actions every time you watch a sports performer. The athlete in Figure 12.2 is straightening his arm as he begins to pull the paddle back through the water. He is therefore extending (joint action) the arm at the elbow (joint).

In examination questions you will normally be expected to state the joint action as well as the type of movement. Remember that there should be two parts to your answer, the joint and the action occurring at it.

ACTION

From the information in this chapter you should be able to answer the following true or false questions.

True or false?

1. The elbow is a hinge joint.
2. The knee is a pivot joint.
3. The elbow is a pivot joint.
4. The shoulder is a pivot joint.
5. The elbow allows flexion and extension.
6. The elbow allows abduction.
7. The hip is a ball and socket joint.
8. The atlas and axis can rotate because they are a hinge joint.
9. All joint actions are possible at the elbow.
10. All joint actions are possible at the hip.
11. The knee is a hinge joint.
12. The atlas and axis can rotate because they are a pivot joint.
13. The shoulder is a ball and socket joint and can rotate.
14. The hip has more movement possibilities that the knee.
15. The elbow has more movement possibilities than the knee.

Figure 12.2 Joint action

ACTION

Name the joint and the joint action occurring at A and B in Figures 12.3 and 12.4.

A

Figure 12.3

B

Figure 12.4

Action	Action at the joint

Table 12.7 Joint actions

ACTION

Try to name some of the joint actions occurring at the knee, elbow, hip and shoulder for the following sporting skills/techniques. You may find it easier to work with a partner – one of you can mime the action, while the other analyses the movement – once finished compare your answers with others.

Skill/technique	Joint	Joint action
Sprint start ('Set')	Knee	
	Hip	
	Elbow	
Stationary, inverted position in a handstand	Knee	
	Elbow	
Kicking the ball in football	Knee	
	Hip	
	Elbow	
Bowling the ball in cricket	Shoulder	
Completing a cartwheel	Elbow	
	Shoulder	

Table 12.2   Joint actions

Extend the table to give joint actions for all four joints. During a practical session you could create a routine that links these movements together and see whether or not your partner can identify them.

(Note that some rotation is permitted at the knee due to the structure of the joint, but the joint actions that you need to remember for the knee are flexion and extension.)

ACTION

Create a revision table by filling in the information missing from Table 12.9.

Joint name	Joint type	Joint action	Example from sport
Knee			
Elbow			
Hip			
Shoulder			
Atlas, axis			

Table 12.9 Revision table

HOMEWORK

Take a photograph of youself performing in sport or taking part in a PE lesson (or use a suitable image from a newspaper). Print your photograph and stick it in the centre of a piece of plain paper. Choose two joints that you are using in the picture and draw a small box around them as shown in Figure 12.5. On your paper, draw the bones as they would appear in the joint, label them, state the name and type of the joint and the action that is happening at the joint in the photograph.

The elbow is a . . .

The knee is a . . .

Figure 12.5

THE MUSCULAR SYSTEM

All sports performers need to be able to move. Movement is possible through the use of muscles, but not all muscles bring about movement.

Classification of muscles

Muscles can be voluntary, involuntary or cardiac. All are essential, but each type fulfils a different role within the body.

Cardiac muscle

Where have you seen this already in the book? Figure 13.1 gives a hint. Cardiac muscle is only found in the heart, and is a special form of involuntary muscle in that we have no

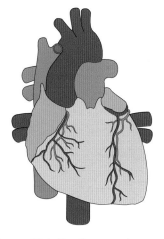

Figure 13.1 Cardiac muscle

direct conscious control over it. It also differs from voluntary muscle in that it does not tire, but continues to contract and relax throughout our lives.

Involuntary muscle

This is found in the walls of organs in the body; eg in the arteries where they control blood flow by altering the size of the internal lumen in the artery (see Chapter 9). This is important to the performer as this will control oxygen delivery.

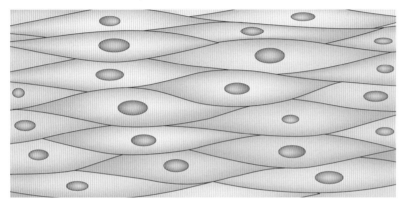

Figure 13.2 Involuntary muscle

Parts of the digestive tract have involuntary muscles, where the action of the muscle contracting squeezes food further along, so it can be digested and essential nutrients extracted for energy for the performer to use.

Involuntary muscles are also responsible for regulating the flow of air through the lungs. Involuntary muscles know when to contract because they react to what is happening within the body. This means that we do not have to consciously control them, as they work on their own.

Voluntary muscle

This is also referred to as skeletal muscle. It is the muscle type responsible for bringing about movement and maintaining body posture. We *do* think about using these muscles – they only move when we ask them to, in other words they are under our conscious control. See Figure 13.5 for the names of the muscles that you need to know for this course.

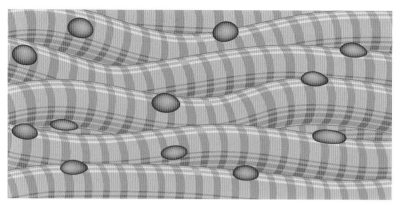

Figure 13.3 Voluntary muscle

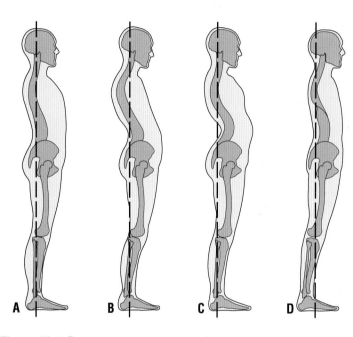

Figure 13.4 Posture

ACTION

Look at the different postures in Figure 13.4. Which is the correct posture? What is wrong with the other images in terms of posture?

Muscle tone

This is one aspect of the use of voluntary muscles that is not controlled consciously. The key point to remember about muscle tone is that

- your voluntary muscles are in a constant state of readiness, through partial contraction; this is what keeps them firm.

Even when relaxed, the muscle is receiving impulses from the brain to stimulate the fibres within the muscle to contract. Muscle tone helps to maintain our posture when standing, sitting and moving. If we have too little muscle tone this can lead to difficulties in balance (important for sports performers); too much muscle tone also has a detrimental effect on performance by making muscles too stiff or rigid to perform movements properly.

Good posture is also important to improve our self image. Sports performers are concerned about having the correct posture as it is the most energy efficient. They need to ensure that they are not 'wasting' energy that could be used to help them perform better.

- Correct posture = A
- Posture B – rounded shoulders, stomach and bottom sticking out
- Posture C – abdomen sticks out in front, back has to arch to compensate to save loss of balance

- Posture D – pelvic girdle leans back, losing natural S shaped curve of vertebral column, body weight is too far forward

Functions of voluntary muscles

Figure 13.5 shows two volleyball players and a closer look at their muscular system.

In order to bring about movement, our muscles contract – they can only pull, not push. They are attached to bones at both ends. One end is fixed and cannot move, so as the muscle contracts, the fixed end (the origin) pulls on the other end of the muscle, which is attached to a different bone. Because this end of the muscle can move (the insertion), it and the bone(s) it is attached to will be pulled towards the other end of the muscle and the bone it is attached to. Look at Figure 13.6 for an example. (Please note: you do not need to know about the origin and insertion of muscles for the exam, but it may help you to know because then you can work out the action of the muscle.)

The biceps are attached to the scapula (origin) and the radius (insertion). Therefore the end of the muscle near the shoulder does not move, but the other end attached to the lower arm does move. When the muscle contracts, the end at the shoulder stays still, but the end attached to the lower arm moves and brings the bones of the lower arm with it – this is flexion at the elbow.

Having completed this movement, how do you move your arm back to its original position? A volleyball player smashing the ball will need flexion at the elbow, but then they will need to extend the arm at the elbow to get ready to dig, set or block the opponent's next shot. By relaxing the biceps and contracting the triceps, the triceps pull the lower arm back down to a straight position. Thus there is:

- flexion of the arm at the elbow caused by the biceps and
- extension of the arm at the elbow brought about by the triceps.

The biceps and triceps are working as an **antagonistic pair**: one muscle contracts while the other relaxes to bring about a movement. The hamstrings and the quadriceps work in the same way.

You should realise that muscle action is complicated, as many muscles often contribute to the action. For your course you should try to focus on the obvious movements that these 11 muscles bring about.

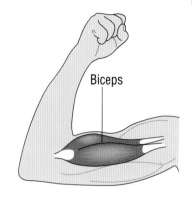

Figure 13.6 The biceps muscle contracts and pulls on the bones of the lower arm

? QUESTION

Looking at the location of the hamstrings, which joint do you think they move? Will they flex or extend the limb around this joint? The answers to this question are in Table 13.1, along with the action of all the other muscles you need to know.

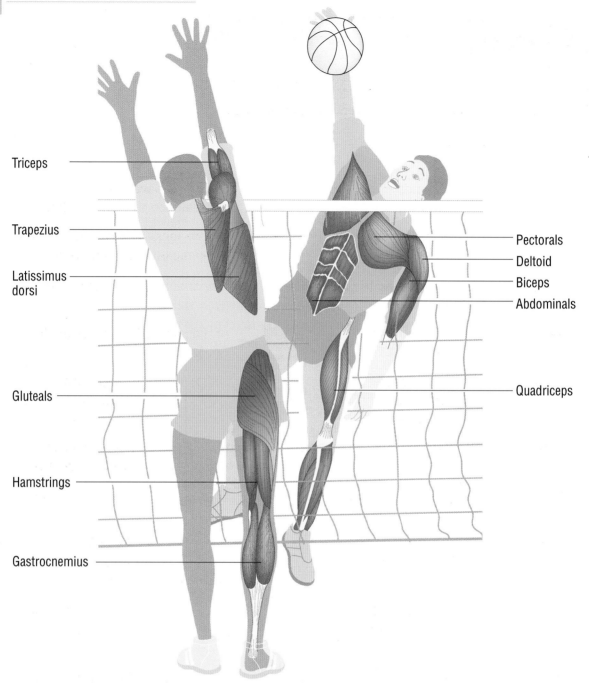

Triceps

Trapezius

Latissimus dorsi

Gluteals

Hamstrings

Gastrocnemius

Pectorals

Deltoid

Biceps

Abdominals

Quadriceps

Figure 13.5 The Muscular System

QUESTION

How many of the muscle names in Figure 13.5 do you know already? There are only 11 to learn, but you need to know what they do as well. Can you work out what any of them do from seeing where they are on the images?

ACTION

Design a weight training programme or a circuit that will exercise all of the muscles identified in Table 13.1.

Muscle	Muscle action	Sporting action
Triceps	Extends lower arm at the elbow	Volleyball player has arms outstretched to block the ball
Biceps	Flexes arm at the elbow	Tennis serve – racket preparation, when racket is behind head
Deltoids	Abducts upper arm at the shoulder	Preparation for a cartwheel in gymnastics
Pectorals	Adduction of upper arm at the shoulder	Arm action in front crawl (pull)
Trapezius	Adducts and rotates scapula, rotation of head at atlas and axis	Lifting of the head to watch the flight of the shuttle in badminton. Back crawl swimming action
Gluteals	Extends the leg at the hip	Running action, one leg is left stretched back behind the other
Quadriceps	Extends the leg at the knee	Follow through after kicking a ball in football
Hamstrings	Flexes the leg at the knee	Tacking the leg back in preparation to strike the ball in a drop goal attempt in rugby
Gastrocnemius	Plantar flexion of the foot (pointing your toes)	Going up onto toes prior to take off in a diving competition
Latissimus dorsi	Adducts and rotates the humerus at the shoulder (draws the arm back and in towards the body)	Pulling the arm back in archery
Abdominals	Flex, rotate and laterally bend trunk	Forward action in sit-ups

Table 13.1 Muscle action and sporting action

Figure 13.7

ACTION

Look at the images in Figure 13.7. Name two of the joints in each image and state the muscle and muscle action that has taken place at that joint.

Isotonic and isometric muscle contractions

Muscles contract when they work. The muscle contractions that we have looked at so far have all resulted in movement, and these types of muscle contraction are called **isotonic** contractions. However, it is possible for a muscle to contract with no resulting movement. These types of contractions are called **isometric** contractions.

Figure 13.8 Isometric contraction

Figure 13.9 Isometric muscle contraction in limbs where muscles are contracting but there is no movement

ACTION

At the end of the previous chapter the homework activity suggested that you make x-ray pictures of your joints in action. Now you can add the names of the muscles causing the joint action.

The only time that muscle contraction will not result in movement is if you are trying to move an immoveable object. For example, if you stand with your arms bent and push them forwards your arms will move as they straighten. This would be an isotonic contraction. If, however, you repeated this exercise, but pushed against a wall, your arms could not straighten because the wall is immoveable. If you try this you will notice that your muscles are still definitely working, and this is an isometric contraction.

In a tug of war, teams will both pull as hard as each other so both team's muscles are working, but if there is no movement they will be contracting isometrically. During a handstand, muscles are working to maintain the position of the body, but there is no movement – this is another example of an isometric muscle contraction.

Slow and fast twitch muscle fibres

Skeletal muscle is made up of fast and slow twitch muscle fibres. The percentage of slow or fast twitch fibres that we have is inherited. Both fibre types have their advantages and disadvantages. A high percentage of fast twitch fibres would give us an advantage in anaerobic activities such as sprinting, whereas a high percentage of slow twitch muscle fibres would give us an advantage in endurance events.

Figure 13.10 Fast twitch fibres are useful in sprinting

Slow twitch fibres are efficient at using oxygen to release energy but are slower to contract than fast twitch fibres, which means that they are not as powerful. Fast twitch fibres can contract quickly, increasing the amount of force that can be exerted by the muscle over a short period of time. The disadvantage with these muscle fibre types is that they tire quickly.

ACTION

The characteristics of the two muscle fibre types make them suitable for different activities. Match the activities listed with the most appropriate muscle fibre type

- sprint start
- sprint finish of 3000 metres
- middle of 3000 metres
- holding a handstand
- elite tennis player serving the ball
- footballer maintaining play over the whole length of the match.

Figure 13.11 Slow twitch fibres are useful in endurance events

Across:

2 In order to move a bone muscles contract. This _____ on one of the bones the muscle is attached to

3 What muscle type is heart muscle an example of?

6 These fibres take a long time to fatigue

10 This muscle type is not attached to the bones of the skeleton

11 This muscle extends the arm at the elbow

14 The deltoid _____ the upper arm at the shoulder

16 Which muscle fibre type works anaerobically? _____ twitch

17 Maintaining good posture is a good idea for athletes because it is more _____ efficient

18 Which muscle type contracts to move bones?

19 Poor _____ often leads to poor posture

Down:

1 Involuntary muscle is found in the _____ of arteries

2 The gastrocnemius allows us to _____ our toes

4 The hamstrings and quadriceps are this

5 Sprinters use these muscle fibre types

7 A tug of war with both sides equal is a good example of _____ muscle contraction

8 This muscle flexes the leg at the knee

9 A disadvantage of fast twitch fibres is that they _____ quickly

12 Rounded _____ is often a sign of poor posture

13 Slow twitch muscle fibres are well suited to _____ activities

15 This word means muscle contraction with movement

Chapter fourteen
TESTING YOUR UNDERSTANDING

Check with your teacher about the course you are following. If at the time of writing you are following the short course you will not need to answer questions on Chaptes 9 to 13; you will also be answering a multiple choice paper, but check, as sometimes these things change! Work through the relevant questions to you, ie only those from the chapters you need to kow, but attempt both full and short course questions (it is good practice). Once you can answer all of the relevant questions in this chapter you will be very well prepared for your final exam. There are two crosswords to finish the chapter. Short course candidates should complete crossword 1, and full course candidates should complete crossword 2.

Chapter 1 (Reasons for taking part in Physical Activity)

1. Hugh is 16 years old. Although he has always enjoyed PE, he is very shy and overweight.

   Complete the table below stating **THREE** possible benefits to Hugh of joining a sports club. Explain how joining a club may achieve these benefits.

	Benefit	How achieved
1		
2		
3		

Possible benefits of taking part in exercise can be grouped as either

A Mental

B Physical

C Social

D Aesthetic

Which of the benefits of exercise named above, **A**, **B**, **C** or **D**, would best match each of the following statements?

2. I participate in exercise to relieve stress.   (1 mark)

3. I joined a local sports club so that I could get out more and meet people.   (1 mark)

4. By taking part in dance I am able to appreciate the skill involved and have become more creative and able to express my ideas.   (1 mark)

5. I restarted my training after Christmas to try to lose weight.   (1 mark)

Chapter 2 (Health, Fitness, Exercise and Performance)

The following are all areas of fitness.

A Muscular strength

B Muscular endurance

C Flexibility

D Cardiovascular fitness

Figure 14.1 shows a badminton player playing a shot.

6. Which area of fitness helps the player stretch to reach the shuttlecock?   (1 mark)

7. Which area of fitness combines with speed to provide the power in the player's shots?   (1 mark)

8. Which area of fitness allows the player to continue to use his arm muscles during long rallies without the muscles becoming fatigued?   (1 mark)

9. a) Give **one** reason why a person may be physically fit but still considered to be unhealthy.

    (1 mark)

    b) Give the correct term for 'how well a task is completed'.

    (1 mark)

Figure 14.1

c) Exercise is 'a form of physical activity done primarily to improve one's health and physical fitness'. How might exercise improve health and fitness?

(i) Health: _____

_____

_____

(1 mark)

(ii) Physical fitness: _____

_____

_____

(1 mark)

(Total 4 marks)

Chapter 3 (Skill Related Fitness)

10. **Figure 14.2** shows performers participating in physical activity.

Figure 14.2

Complete the table below naming **ONE** component of skill-related fitness that will be important to each performer. Explain how these components will help each performer in his/her activity. You **must** choose a different component for each performer.

Performer	Component of skill-related fitness	How component of skill-related fitness helps performance
A: GYNMAST		
B: SPRINTER		
C: SHOT PUTTER		

(Total 6 marks)

The following are all areas of skill-related fitness.

A Coordination

B Reaction time

C Speed

D Power

The following statements explain how Najeeb, a 100 metre sprinter, uses all of the areas of skill-related fitness, **A**, **B**, **C** and **D**. Match each statement with the correct area of skill-releated fitness.

11. To help him drive out of the starting blocks at the start of the race.

(1 mark)

12. To use his arms and legs together to create a better running action.

(1 mark)

13. To make sure he leaves the blocks as soon as possible after the gun has sounded.

(1 mark)

14. To complete a race faster than his opponent.

(1 mark)

Chapter 4 (Principles of Training)

15. To improve performance, athletes often work on their fitness. In order to be effective, performers should devise a Personal Exercise Programme (PEP). Shiraz is 16, and plays sport at a good standard. The following is an extract of some of his thoughts about his PEP:

Extract from Shiraz's Personal Exercise Programme,

At present I'm training three times a week, every week, but at first I only went once a week. I use a different method of training for each session, but I make sure that I focus on appropriate tasks for my activity. At the end of each session I plan the next one, gradually increasing the amount of work I do when I think its getting too easy.

a) From the extract state **five** Principles of Training that Shiraz applies:

(i) _____

(ii) _____

(iii) _____

(iv) _____

(v) _____

(5 marks)

b) For each Principle of Training that you have identified, give an example from the extract to support your answer.

Principle of Training	Example from extract
(i)	
(ii)	
(iii)	
(iv)	
(v)	

(5 marks)

c) Why does Shiraz design his own PEP rather than using the same programme as one of his friends?

(1 mark)
(Total 11 marks)

The following statments all relate to the **FITT** principle.

A How hard you work.

B Making sure that your training matches the needs of your sport.

C How long each training session lasts.

D How often you train.

16. Which of these statements is referring to **Frequency**?

17. Which of these statements is referring to **Type**?

18. Which of these statements is referring to **Intensity**?

(3 marks)

The following statements are taken from a GCSE PE student's Personal Exercise Programme (PEP).

A I found the workload far too easy last week so I shall be training harder this week.

B I think it is important to gradually increase the amount of work that I do.

C I need to structure my PEP to my needs, no one else's.

D Unfortunately I had to have a minor operation on my knee. I was unable to train for six weeks, which means that I have already started to lose my fitness.

19. Which statement refers to the principle of progression?

20. Which statement refers to the principle of reversibility?

(2 marks)

Chapter 5 (Methods of Training)

21. **Fartlek**, **circuit**, **weight** and **interval** are all types of training methods.

   a) Briefly describe each type of training method.

   Fartlek: _____

   _____

   Circuit: _____

   _____

   Weight: _____

   _____

   Interval: _____

   _____

(4 marks)

   b) Look at the following list of sporting performers.

Hockey player	Football midfield player
Tennis player	Competitive swimmer
Shot putter	Rower
Sprinter	Netball shooter

   Complete the following table by selecting the **most** appropriate performer from the table above for each type of training. Each performer may only be used **once**.

Type of training	Sports performer
Fartlek	
Circuit	
Weight	
Interval	

(4 marks)

c) Explain why the training method is of value to the sports performer that you have chosen.

Type of training	Value of training method to sporting activity
Fartlek	
Circuit	
Weight	
Interval	

(4 marks)
(Total 12 marks)

Figure 14.3 shows a record of Jane's heart rate before, during and after a training session.

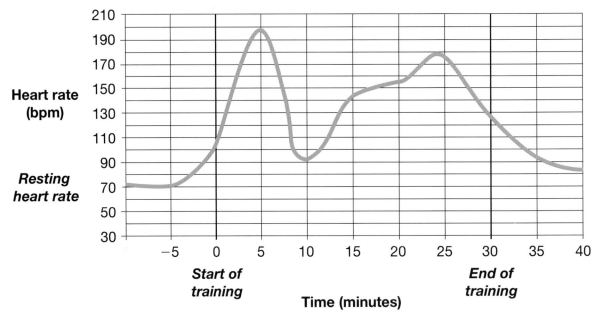

Figure 14.3

Questions **22** to **24** relate to the information in Figure 14.3.

22. Why does Jane's heart rate drop during the training session?

 A She becomes tired.

 B She increases her workload.

 C She decreases her workload.

 D She maintains the same workload.

(1 mark)

23. How long does it take Jane to recover?

    A She recovers immediately.

    B One minute.

    C Less than 5 minutes.

    D More than 5 minutes.

    (1 mark)

24. If Jane's **target heart rate training zones** were to be added to the graph, what percentages of her maximum heart rate should be used to calculate her target heart rate training zones?

    A 50% and 60%

    B 55% and 65%

    C 60% and 80%

    D 70% and 100%

    (1 mark)

Chapter 6 (Diet, Health and Hygiene)

The following nutrients should all be present in a balanced diet.

A Protein

B Fats

C Carbohydrates

D Water

25. Which of these provides energy for anaerobic respiration?

    (1 mark)

26. If eaten in excess, which of these is most likely to lead to obesity?

    (1 mark)

27. Which of these are required to reduce the chances of becoming dehydrated?

The following are all possible side effects from taking illegal, performance-enhancing drugs.

A Dehydration

B Acne

C Increased chance of injury

D Increased chance of heart disease

    (1 mark)

28. Which of these is a possible side effect of taking **narcotic analgesics**?

29. a) In addition to keeping fit, Ashan also knows that it is important to consider what and how much he eats.

   Why would Ashan include the following in his diet?

   i) Carbohydrates _____

   (1 mark)

   ii) Water _____

   (1 mark)

30. Why is it important that Ashan does not **under eat**?

   (1 mark)

31. It is important that Ashan does not over eat. Explain the term **over eat**.

   (1 mark)

Chapter 7 (Prevention of Injury)

32. What is the purpose of 'balancing competition'?

   A To see which gymnastics team can hold a position for the longest.

   B To try to even out sides within a competition.

   C To make sure that the cost of running a competition does not exceed the money generated from ticket sales.

   D To see which gymnast can use the most balances within their competition routine.

   (1 mark)

The following statements are extracts taken from a football player's Personal Exercise Programme.

   A As I arrived late I had no time to warm up properly.

   B I made sure I remembered my shin pads for this game.

   C Before making the substitution the referee checked the studs on my boots to make sure they were not too long or made of metal.

   D After the match I made sure I had a shower before going home.

33. Which statement should reduce the chance of injury to an opponent?

   (1 mark)

34. Which statement should reduce the chance of injury to the football player?

   (1 mark)

35. a) One way of attempting to prevent injury is to 'play by the rules'. Complete the table below by giving **two** examples from a sporting activity of your choice to show how 'rules' may prevent injury.

ACTIVITY: _____

Description of rule	How rule reduces chance of injury

(2 marks)

b) i) Different activities create different levels of risk for the performers.

Which of the following activities presents the greatest risk?

Basketball – Weight Training – 1500m – Rock Climbing

_____

(1 mark)

ii) Explain your answer.

_____

_____

(1 mark)

c) Complete the table below by giving a potential risk and precaution that could be taken to reduce that risk. Each risk and precaution may only be used once.

Activity	Potential risk	Measure to reduce risk
Basketball		
Weight Training		
1500m		
Rock Climbing		

(8 marks)
(Total 12 marks)

Chapter 8 (Sports Injury)

The following conditions can relate to sports injuries.

A Unconscious

B No pulse

C Broken leg

D Torn ligament

36. Which of these conditions would result in the casualty receiving cardiac massage?

(1 mark)

37. Which of these is a soft tissue injury?

(1 mark)

38. Which of these conditions would result in the casualty being placed in the recovery position?

(1 mark)

39. During a recent competition one of the hurdlers fell and sprained her ankle.

   i)   State **ONE visible** symptom of a sprained ankle.

   _____

(1 mark)

   ii) What type of injury is a sprained ankle?

   _____

(1 mark)

   iii) What treatment should she be given for this type of injury?

   _____

(1 mark)
(Total 3 marks)

Chapter 9 (The Cardiovascular System (Circulatory system))

40. Platelets are responsible for:

   A Fighting infection

   B Carrying oxygen

   C Clotting

   D Carrying carbon dioxide

(1 mark)

41. Stroke volume is:

    A The amount of blood ejected from the heart per minute
    B The number of times the heart beats per minute
    C The amount of blood ejected from the heart per beat
    D The pace-maker responsible for timing the stroke of the heart

                                                    (1 mark)

42. **Figure 14.4** is a diagram of the human heart.

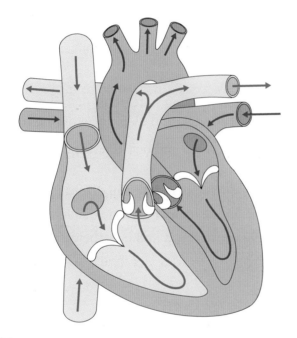

Figure 14.4

    a) Name the parts labelled **A**, **B** and **C**.

        i)   **A** _____
                                                    (1 mark)

        ii) **B** _____
                                                    (1 mark)

        iii) **C** _____
                                                    (1 mark)

    b) Why do the walls of the vessel labelled **A** need to be thicker than those labelled **C**?

        _____
                                                    (1 mark)
                                            (Total 4 marks)

Chapter 10 (The Respiratory System)

43. Vital capacity is:

    A The amount of air breathed in and out during normal breathing

    B The largest volume of air which can be expired after the deepest possible inspiration

    C The amount of air moving in and out of the lungs in one minute

    D The amount of air that stays in the lungs after the maximum expiration

    Answer: _____

    (1 mark)

44. Which of the following statements describes the movement of the ribs and diaphragm during inspiration?

    A The ribs move up and out, the diaphragm moves down

    B The ribs move up and in, the diaphragm moves down

    C The ribs move up and out, the diaphragm moves up

    D The ribs move down and out, the diaphragm moves down

    Answer: _____

    (1 mark)

Chapter 11 (The Skeletal System (Bones))

45. The skeleton provides support and gives us our shape.

    a) State **two other** functions of the skeleton and relate them to sporting examples.

    Function 1: _____

    Relevance to sport: _____

    Example from sport: _____

    _____

    Function 2: _____

    Relevance to sport: _____

    Example from sport: _____

    _____

    (6 marks)

b) Bones develop through a process called ossification. In which part of the bone does growth take place?

_____

_____

(1 mark)

c) How might the length of a performer's limbs affect the sport they choose to play?

_____

_____

(1 mark)

(Total 8 marks)

Question 46 should be answered by writing **A**, **B**, **C** or **D** in the space provided.

46. Which of the following groups contain the bones of the hand **and** wrist?

A Tibia, Tarsals, Phalanges

B Tarsals, Metatarsals, Phalanges

C Clavicle, Metatarsals, Tarsals

D Carpals, Phalanges, Metacarpals

Answer: _____

(1 mark)

Chapter 12 (Joints and Ligaments)

47. Bones in other areas of the skeleton meet to form important joints, for example, the knee.

i) What type of synovial joint is the knee?

_____

(1 mark)

ii) There can be very slight rotation or sideways movement at the knee joint. What **stabilises** the knee joint to prevent unwanted movement?

_____

(1 mark)

iii) As well as slight rotation, what are the **TWO** types of movement possible at the knee?

1. _____

2. _____

(2 marks)

(Total 4 marks)

48. Which of the following statements best describes a function of ligaments?

 A Provides movement for the joint

 B Provides joint stability

 C Provides a point of muscle attachment to bones

 D Provides protection for the surface of the bones

_____

(1 mark)

Chapter 13 (Muscles)

49. a) Which of the following terms is the correct muscle type for the biceps?

 A Voluntary

 B Fast twitch

 C Slow twitch

 D Involuntary

_____

(1 mark)

 b) Which muscle, **A**, **B** or **C**, allows the runner to drive fowards off the toes during his running action?

_____

(1 mark)

 c) Which muscle, **A**, **B** or **C**, allows the runner to extend the leg at the hip?

_____

(1 mark)

 d) Two of the muscles named in the box below work as an **antagonistic pair**. Name the two muscles.

Bicep   Hamstrings   Deltoid   Quadriceps   Gluteals

_____ and _____

(1 mark)

 e) Explain the term 'antagonistic pair'.

_____

_____

(1 mark)
(Total 5 marks)

50. Figure 14.5 is a diagram of the human muscular system from the front and the back.

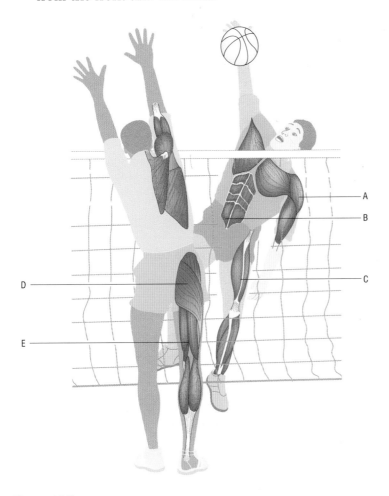

Figure 14.5

For each of the muscles A to E (shown in Figure 14.5) select the **most** appropriate action from the box below to show its use in sport. Each action may only be used **once**.

(5 marks)

(1) Arm action when preparing to start a cartwheel

(2) Extending the arm into the water during the front crawl action

(3) The downward phase of a press up

(4) The follow through after kicking a ball

(5) The upward phase of a press up

(6) Taking the leg back at the hip in preparation to kick a ball

(7) A pike in trampolining

(8) Legs bent in preparation for a sprint start

Muscle	Action/Action number
A	
B	
C	
D	
E	

51. **Figure 14.6** shows the legs of a runner.

(Total 8 marks)

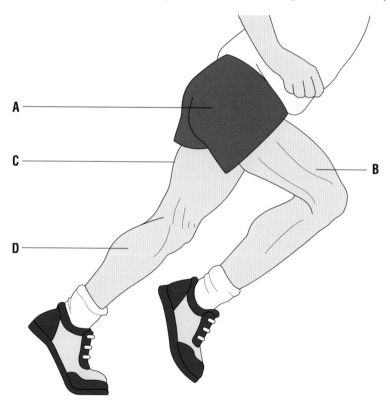

Figure 14.6

Label the muscles **A**, **B** and **C**.

A _____

B _____

C _____

D _____

(4 marks)

REVISION CROSSWORD FOR SHORT COURSE

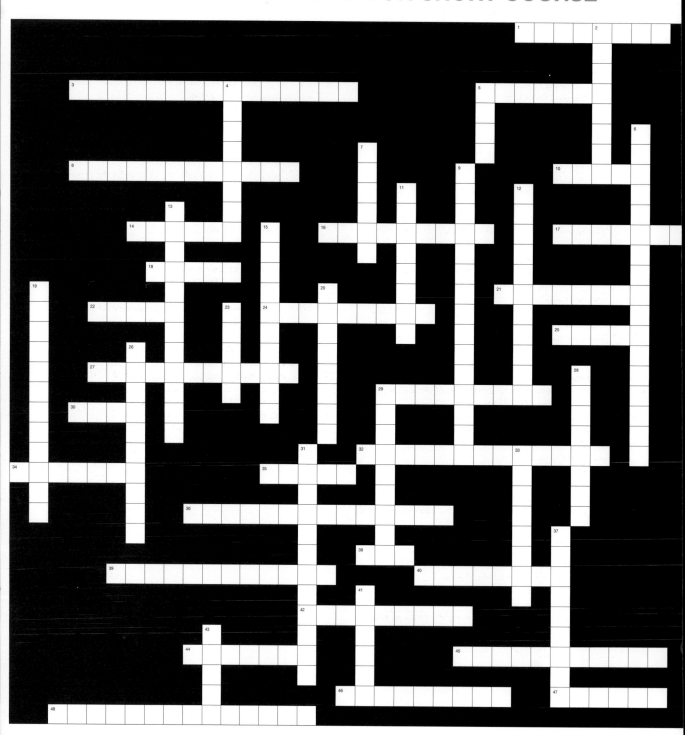

CLUES FOR REVISION CROSSWORD FOR SHORT COURSE ON PREVIOUS PAGE

Across

1. Studs in boots help reduce the risk of injury by reducing the risk of the player
3. A drop in resting heart rate is an effect of _____
5. Exercise is good for us because it can improve our health and _____
8. What phase is missing from the following exercise session? Warm up _____ Cool down
10. What are used to try to reduce the chance of injury?
14. Athletes eat carbohydrates to provide them with _____
16. Activity that means working without oxygen
17. Suitable training method for games players
18. A dislocation is an example of a _____ injury
21. Which sports injury is being described? 'A crack or break in the bone'
22. What is the missing component of a balanced diet? Fat, carbohydrates, vitamins, minerals, protein and water
24. If you need to overload you must increase the _____ of the exercise session
25. What component of fitness does the sprinter need to reach the finish line first?
27. Which principle of training tells you to increase your work load gradually?
29. Blood doping _____ red blood cell count
30. How many components of health-related exercise are there?
32. Which principle of training is this an example of? Last time I trained I could lift 20 kg, this time I lifted 15 kg
34. Type of training method arranged into stations
35. We should wash after exercise to remove _____
36. A rugby player swerving past opponents uses _____ to make sure he stays on his feet
38. Is it possible to be fit but not healthy?
39. Javelin throwers need this to time the movement of their feet and arms correctly to produce a good throw
40. An example of protective clothing for a hockey player would be _____
42. If I'm working at 70% of my maximum heart rate, I'm said to be working in my _____ of training
44. 220 is the recognised _____ heart rate
45. Water is important to reduce the chance of _____
46. _____ athletes are more likely to take EPO than performers in other types of activities
47. What is being defined? 'A state of complete physical, social and mental well being'
48. This aspect of fitness relates to the heart, blood and blood vessels

Down

2. Weight loss is an example of a _____ benefit of exercise
4. What is the name of the position you place someone in if they are breathing and have a pulse?
5. Balancing competition should make the competition _____
6. What aspect of fitness am I trying to improve? 'I lift light weights every other day and do 4 sets of 15 reps'
7. Reason for taking part in physical activity
9. Which principle of training tells you to consider the person when planning a training session?
11. What aspect of fitness is being used? 'I hit the ball hard for a six'
12. A warm up increases body _____
13. The time it takes for your body to return to its resting state is called your _____
15. Training sessions without breaks
19. Psychological benefit of taking part in physical activity
20. Alcohol intake slows these
23. Type of training method that allows you to vary the training method you are using for different sessions
26. Which principle of training is missing? FIR_____STOP
28. An example of an aerobic event
29. Increased heart rate is an _____ effect of exercise
31. This component of skill-related fitness is essential at the start of the race for swimmers and sprint runners
33. Good training method for sprinters
37. Extreme body type associated with sprinters
41. A strain is damage to a _____ or muscle
43. Boxers use gloves to stop them hurting their _____ as much

REVISION CROSSWORD FOR FULL COURSE

CLUES FOR REVISION CROSSWORD FOR FULL COURSE ON PREVIOUS PAGE

Across

1. The time it takes for your body to return to its resting state is called your _____
2. Type of training method that allows you to vary the training methods you are using for different sessions
6. _____ are the link between the larger blood vessels
7. Type of training method arranged into stations
8. A drop in resting heart rate is an effect of _____
11. A rugby player swerving past opponents uses _____ to make sure he stays on his feet
13. This is one of the functions of the skeleton
14. Psychological benefit of taking part in physical activity
15. 220 is the recognised _____ heart rate
21. Which type of joint gives the greatest range of movement?
23. Good training method for sprinters
24. An example of protective clothing for a hockey player would be
27. Which principle of training is this an example of? 'Last time I trained I could lift 20 kg, this time I lifted 15 kg'
28. Which principle of training tells you to increase your work load gradually?
29. Which muscle extends the leg at the hip?
36. Alcohol intake slows these
39. How many components of health-related exercise are there?
40. A warm up increases body _____
41. What divides the heart in two to prevent the mixing of oxygenated and deoxygenated blood?
43. Javelin throwers need this to time the movement of their feet and arms correctly to produce a good throw
45. A dislocation is an example of a _____ injury
47. We should wash after exercise to remove _____
49. Blood doping _____ red blood cell count
52. What are used to try to reduce the chance of injury?
53. Tendons attach to _____ and bone
55. This is produced during anaerobic activity
58. What component of fitness does the sprinter need to reach the finish line first?
59. What aspect of fitness is being used? 'I hit the ball hard for a six'
60. The knee is an example of what type of joint?
61. This aspect of fitness relates to the heart, blood and blood vessels
65. Which principle of training tells you to consider the person when planning a training session?
66. If the muscles are contracting but there is no limb movement, what type of muscle contraction is taking place?
67. Extreme body type associated with sprinters
68. Water is important to reduce the chance of _____
69. The action of bringing the arm back towards the centre of the body from the side is called _____
70. If I am working at 70% of my maximum heart rate I am said to be working in my _____ of training
71. Which bone type acts as a lever?
72. Exercise is good for us because it can improve our health and _____
73. What is the name of the position you place someone in if they are breathing and have a pulse?

Down

1. This component of skill-related fitness is essential at the start of the race for swimmers and sprint runners
3. If we increase this we can increase our cardiac output
4. What phase is missing from the following exercise session? Warm up _____ Cool down
5. Which muscle pulls your arms back and in towards the body?
9. Balancing competition should make the competition _____
10. What is the missing component of a balanced diet? Fat, carbohydrates, vitamins, minerals, protein and water
12. Weight loss is an example of a _____ benefit of exercise
16. The ribs move like this when we inspire
17. Which area of the vertebral column is designed to support the body weight?
18. Increased heart rate is an _____ effect of exercise
19. _____ athletes are more likely to take EPO than performers in other types of activities
20. What is the term given to muscles that work together to allow a limb to move?
22. Reason for taking part in physical activity
25. Boxers use gloves to stop them hurting their _____ as much
26. Which chamber of the heart has the thickest muscular wall?
30. This is the place where gas exchange occurs in the lungs
31. A joint is a place where two or more bones _____
32. A strain is damage to a _____ or muscle
33. What type of blood does the left atrium receive?
34. Athletes eat carbohydrates to provide them with _____
35. Is it possible to be fit but not healthy?
37. What is being defined? 'A state of complete physical, social and mental well being'
38. Suitable training method for games players
39. What sports injury is being described? A crack or break in the bone
42. Activity that means working without oxygen
44. Regular training can increase _____ volume
48. What is the missing muscle type? Voluntary and involuntary
50. An example of an aerobic event
51. Which principle of training is missing? FIR _____ STOP
54. Which is the missing gas? Oxygen and nitrogen
56. If you need to overload you must increase the _____ of the exercise session
57. Training session without breaks
62. The scapula is an example of what type of bone?
63. Studs in boots help reduce the risk of injury by reducing the risk of the player _____
64. What is the muscle type of our skeletal muscles?

GLOSSARY

Some of the terms used in the book are explained below. If the term you are looking for is not in the glossary, this is probably because it is explained in sufficient detail in the book. It must be emphasised that these are EXPLANATIONS of the terms to help you understand their meanings. The definitions you require for your examination can be found within the chapters of the book rather than in the glossary.

Aerobic — Where performers use oxygen to release energy, eg endurance athletes

Aesthetic appreciation — Appreciating the beauty of a skilful performance. This does not just mean in activities like gymnastics or dance; it is equally valid when watching skilful play in games such as rugby or football

Alveoli — Air sacks found in the lungs, where the exchange of gases takes place

Anaerobically — Working at a high work rate so there is not enough time to release energy using oxygen. Therefore, working 'without oxygen'

Antagonistic pair — This is where muscles are used in connection with one another to bring about certain movements. For example, the triceps will relax to allow the biceps to contract. This results in flexion of arm at the elbow. If the bicep relaxes, this allows the triceps to contract to extend the arm at the elbow.

Balanced diet — Daily intake of the right foods to provide the body with all that it needs for energy, growth and repair

Biomechanical aspects of respiration — How the body operates to bring about breathing, in other words the role of the muscles to bring about the movement of the skeleton to make breathing possible

Blood doping — Removal and later re-infusion of a performer's blood to increase the oxygen-carrying capacity of the blood and therefore improve performance in aerobic activities

Blood pressure — Usually 120/80. Refers to the resistance to blood flow as the blood passes through the arteries

Capillarisation — Increase in the number of capillaries as a result of aerobic training, allowing greater exchange of gases between the blood and the muscles

Cardiac hypertrophy — Increase in size of heart muscle. Effect of regular training

Cardiac massage	Also known as heart massage, it is the rhythmic compression of the chest and heart in an attempt to maintain blood flow after heart failure
Cardiac output	The amount of blood leaving the heart per minute
Cardiovascular system	Heart, blood and blood vessels
Central nervous system	The brain and spinal cord, responsible for the coordination and control of the nervous system
Classification	A way of deciding if items go together in a group. For example, bones can be classified or grouped as long, short, flat or irregular
Components	Bits or parts that make up something. For example, the components of a joint are the parts of the joint: tendons, ligaments, muscle, joint capsule and so on
Cool down	What you should do after exercise to help return the body to its resting state. It involves slow jogging and stretching
CPR	Cardiopulmonary resuscitation. A combination of cardiac massage and artificial respiration used to maintain the circulation of oxygenated blood to the brain
Deoxygenated blood	Blood that has circulated the body and 'delivered' its oxygen to the tissues
Diaphragm	Muscle used in breathing
Diffusion	Movement of gases from a high concentration to a low concentration
Elite performers	Individuals who have trained to become among the best at their sport
Energy	The body needs this to be able to carry out physical work. The harder we train, the more energy we need
EPO	This is something which occurs naturally in the body, but is now being made and sold to performers as illegal performance-enhancing drugs. Its full name is erythopoietin. Like blood doping it increases the oxygen-carrying capacity of the blood
Expired air	What you breath out
Fatigue	When the body, or part of it, becomes tired
Function	Job or role. For example, one of the functions of the skeleton is to protect the vital organs
Gaseous exchange	The swapping of oxygen and carbon dioxide due to the pressure gradients of each of the gases at the site of the exchange
Haemoglobin	Substance in red blood cells that allows transportation of oxygen
Immediate effects of exercise	What happens to your body as soon as you start to do any physical work. For example, increase in heart rate
Inspired air	What you breath in
Lactic acid	Formed by the body during anaerobic exercise
Long-term benefits of exercise	The possible physical improvements in your health as a result of following a regular training programme.

	For example, drop in blood pressure
Lumen	The internal cavity within blood vessels
Maximal	Working flat out (maximum intensity). For example, sprinters work maximally in their event
Mitochondria	Found in muscles, the site of aerobic respiration
Muscular hypertrophy	Increase in muscle size. Effect of regular training
Myoglobin	Acts as an oxygen store in the muscles. Oxygen leaves haemoglobin in blood for myoglobin in the muscles
Oxygen debt	The amount of oxygen consumed during recovery above that which would have been normally used at rest. It is produced because of a shortfall in availability of oxygen during exercise
Oxygenated blood	Blood that has 'collected' oxygen from the lungs and not yet travelled around the body and had the oxygen removed
PEP	Personal Exercise Programme. You should be designing one of these as part of your practical work. It is a training programme designed specifically for you
Performance-enhancing drugs	Illegal drugs used to improve performance
Regular training effects	Changes that happen to your body after following an exercise programme for a period of weeks. For example, a drop in the resting heart rate due to increased strength of cardiac muscle

Rehabilitation	Period of recovery after injury or ill health
Symptoms	A sign or an indication of the existence of something else. For example, a sign or symptom of a fracture is difficulty in moving the injured limb
Target zones	The area between the minimum and maximum threshold of training
Threshold of training	A threshold is a line. Maximum threshold is a line you do not want to cross, and is 80 per cent of your maximum heart rate. Minimum threshold is also a line you do not want to cross, and is 60 per cent of your maximum heart rate. If you stay between these two lines (within your target zone), your training is likely to be more effective
Tidal volume	Amount of air moved into and out of the lungs per breath (normal breathing)
Ventilation	Movement of air into and out of the lungs
Vertebral column	Bones that run down the back (spine)
Vital capacity	The amount of air that can be forcibly breathed out after breathing in as big a breath as possible
Warm up	What you should do before exercise to prepare the body and mind for activity. It involves jogging, stretching and drills related to the main session

INDEX